T0338151

Jens Jensen

Writings Inspired by Nature

Jens Jensen

Writings Inspired by Nature

EDITED BY
WILLIAM H. TISHLER

WISCONSIN HISTORICAL SOCIETY PRESS

Published by the Wisconsin Historical Society Press
Publishers since 1855

wisconsinhistory.org

Photographs identified with WHi or WHS are from the Society's collections; address requests to
reproduce these photos to the Visual Materials Archivist at the Wisconsin Historical Society, 816 State Street,
Madison, WI 53706.

Photo page ii: Jens Jensen at the fountain he designed for Indiana Dunes State Park, circa 1930s, courtesy
Prairie Club Archives, Westchester Township History Museum, Chesterton, Indiana. Pages vi–vii and
154–155: Proposed Improvements Humboldt Park, ca. 1907 plan, courtesy of Chicago Park District Special
Collections. Plan pages 2–3: Jens Jensen papers and drawings, Chi Parks 35, Bentley Historical Library,
University of Michigan.

"Natural Parks and Gardens" is © SEPS licensed by Curtis Licensing, Indianapolis, IN. All rights reserved.

Printed in Canada
Designed by Steve Biel

16 15 14 13 12   1 2 3 4 5

Library of Congress Cataloging-in-Publication Data

Jensen, Jens, 1860–1951.
  Jens Jensen : writings inspired by nature / edited by William H. Tishler.
    p. cm.
  Includes bibliographical references and index.
  ISBN 978-0-87020-490-6 (hardcover : alk. paper) 1. Landscape architecture—Middle West—History—
20th century. 2. Landscape protection—Middle West—History—20th century. 3. Nature conservation—
Middle West—History—20th century. 4. Landscape ecology—Middle West—History—20th century.
5. Human ecology—Middle West—History—20th century. 6. Philosophy of nature—Middle West—
History—20th century. 7. Middle West—Environmental conditions—History—20th century. I. Tishler,
William H. II. Title.
  SB470.54.M54J46 2012
  712.0972—dc23
                            2012007289

Publication of this book was made possible in part by gifts from John K. Notz Jr., Bruce Johnson, and The Kubly Foundation.

MUSIC

COURT

HITCHING
PLACE.

PERGOLA

MALL

GARDEN
GATE

PROPOSED IMPROVEMENTS
IN
HUMBOLDT PARK

DIVISION ST.

Contents

Jensen during the planning and construction phase of
Lincoln Memorial Garden, Springfield, Illinois, circa 1938

Courtesy of Lincoln Memorial Garden Archives

INTRODUCTION

by William H. Tishler

*"We can still see him in his late eighties, erect and vigorous,
standing under a tall pine on his beloved estate while inveighing, his face
looking like a storm cloud, against the cruelties, the greed, the injustice,
the social ignorance, the sordidness and the exploitation of human
beings in man's profit world. Then his face would brighten, it would fill
with humor and kindliness while he would tell of the joys and the
compensations that come to the person who lives in close communion
with Nature and observes her laws."*

—*William T. Evjue*[1]

Jens Jensen is regarded as one of the greatest landscape architects of his age. This reputation is based primarily on his extensive work as a designer of a variety of landscapes throughout the Midwest and beyond. At the time of his death in 1951, Jensen had achieved considerable notoriety and the *New York Times* called him the "dean of American landscape architecture."[2]

Born in 1860 to affluent farmers in Dybbøl, Denmark, Jensen immigrated to America when he was twenty-four in part to escape the German occupation of his homeland and also in response to his family's refusal to accept his fiancée, Anna Marie Hansen. Having personally experienced Prussian imperialism and militarism, he wished to be free of the feudal obligations and aristocratic authoritarianism in Denmark—and to marry against his family's wishes.

Once in the United States Jensen earned a living on farms in Florida and Iowa. He and Anna Marie then moved to Chicago, where he found work in a soap factory before starting as a street sweeper within the West Park System. His fascination with the area's natural features would shape his design philosophy, which was based on native plants and other aspects of the Midwest's environment. In 1894 Jensen rose to become superintendent of Chicago's Humboldt Park and held that position until 1900, when he was dismissed for refusing to participate in political graft. He then began his own design practice. Rehired in 1905 as superintendent of the entire West Park System, Jensen shifted his role to consulting landscape architect in 1909, a position he held until 1921. He became a major figure in Chicago's cultural life during this time. His private practice designing gardens, estates, and parks throughout the Midwest and beyond—often for some of the region's most prominent citizens— flourished. At the same time he established a reputation as a well-known and outspoken conservationist.

Jensen was also a prolific and visionary writer. Yet, with the exception of his two books, *Siftings* and *The Clearing*, too little is known about his many published works.[3] Throughout his illustrious career he wrote articles for gardening magazines and national publications, newsletters for conservation and civic groups, planning reports, and pieces for scores of newspapers, plus countless letters to friends, colleagues, editors, politicians, government officials, civic activists, and environmentalists.

This book is a collection of many of Jensen's most significant essays. They are presented with their often-unconventional spellings and grammar and arranged chronologically to help the reader follow the maturation of his thinking and writing style. They also provide important insights into how his philosophy of working with a landscape's sense of place—especially its native plants—evolved during his long, thought-provoking career.

Like the noted English landscape designer Andre Repton, who spread his ideas through his "Red Books," or Andrew Jackson Downing, who founded the *Horticulturist* and authored several influential books on rural architecture and American landscape gardening, Jensen realized the power of the printed word for disseminating his views about conservation, planning, and landscape design. He believed that his approach to design should be a universal philosophy for shaping outdoor spaces; thus, he zealously shared his ideas for working with a wide range of landscapes, from home gardens to cities to large areas of countryside.

"I believe in the influence that environments exert on humans, both for the good and the bad," Jensen wrote.[4] He considered the experience of environment to be a paramount determinant in shaping human behavior and character. Given this belief, he acted to improve built environments and worked to save prime areas of the natural world, including wilderness areas and native landscapes of North America. He was an environmentalist long before the term became popular during the 1960s.

Jensen's published essays chronicle the growth of a true artist concerned not with egoistic expression but rather the overall destiny of the individual and the greater cultural advancement of humanity. He did not discriminate in his empathy. His work enriched the lives of aristocratic estate owners such as Henry Ford, for whom he designed the grounds of Fair Lane in Dearborn, Michigan, as well as the working class and poor through his decades-long advocacy for public parks on Chicago's West Side. He was a creative and progressive thinker with a fundamental belief that the grandest landscapes of North America should be preserved for future generations of all citizens.

Jensen's writings are best represented not as distinct categories of interest or as periods in the life of an artist, philosopher, conservationist, educator, or social critic. Rather, when regarded as a body of work, they appear to be an interwoven collection of repeated themes and parable-like anecdotes of wisdom received from the soil by the master landscape designer.

This education from the soil was the subject of Jensen's first book, *Siftings*, published in 1939 and republished in 1990.[5] Its collection of stories about his youth and personal philosophy based on the land reveal much about his thoughts on landscape design and American culture. These writings, plus his thoughts about life, conservation, and the powerful influence of landscapes, were included in his second book, *The Clearing*, written ten years later. Both were then reprinted, along with a new chapter, "The Preservation of Our River Courses and Their Natural Setting," in *Siftings, the Major Portion of The Clearing, and Collected Writings*, published posthumously in 1956 by Ralph Fletcher Seymour.[6] Leonard Eaton's biography of Jens Jensen, *Landscape Artist in America*, completed in 1964, incorporated quotations from Jensen's writings and letters to clients with photographs, drawings of some of Jensen's landscape designs, and Eaton's scholarly interpretation of Jensen's work.[7] More recently Robert Grese's popular *Jens Jensen: Maker of Natural Parks and Gardens*, published in 1992, remains a classic work about Jensen and his career.[8]

Jensen published his first articles as early as 1899 in *Park and Cemetery* magazine.[9] This monthly publication from Chicago featured a wide variety of landscape topics. Most of Jensen's early essays were horticultural in scope and ranged from moving and planting large trees to recommending the use of nonnative ornamental plants such as Japanese magnolia, mollis azaleas, and Russian olive. They reveal that his design philosophy and insistence on using native species developed over time and was never absolute; he sometimes used nonnative plants such as lilacs, which he referred to as "pets."[10] His writing also began to express his growing knowledge about the relationships between plants and the landscape. "Extermination of the Oak at Lake Geneva, Wisconsin," for example, was an article based on his astute observations from working more than a decade with landscape projects.[11]

Shortly after the turn of the century, Jensen began to explain his early design rationale in "Plan for Hospital Grounds." This garden plan, for St. Ann's Hospital in Chicago, included areas for exercise to help treat patients with consumption. In this environment, he noted, "every added attraction would prove of great benefit to the patient-visitor."[12]

In "Topiary Gardening," Jensen expressed his dislike of imitation, whether it was the "distortion of tree growth" into "freaks" or American garden designers replicating European styles.[13] Noting the folly of creating an Italian garden in America, he wrote, "These gardens had their origin in southern countries and only there attain their true character."[14] This was Jensen's first published call for regionally based landscape designs, and it revealed his sensitivity to the uniqueness of the North American environment.

After his early articles in *Park and Cemetery*, Jensen began addressing topics of broader social significance. Following his dismissal as superintendent at Humboldt Park he penned "Parks and Politics," a strong statement of his thoughts and concerns regarding the park movement at the turn of the century.[15] The essay focused on problems created by politicized park "mismanagement," which he experienced firsthand at Chicago's West Park System. He presented this paper at the Boston convention of the American Park and Outdoor Art Association, and it was published twice in 1902, in the organization's *Proceedings* and as a reprint in *Park and Cemetery*. As Jensen stated:

> *Political supervision tends to destroy the beauty of our parks, promotes the carrying out of inartistic and useless improvements . . . and squanders public money; and they do not create for the city what originally was intended—a beautiful park, a lasting monument of nature and art, a practical demonstration of culture and refinement, to which the municipality may point with pride and honor.*[16]

These early articles contain hints of Jensen's emerging character and artistry that began appearing between 1902 and 1906. In this four-year span he published seven articles, some containing early statements of important themes that would underlie his work for the rest of his career as a landscape architect.[17] In one of these, "Urban and Suburban Landscape Gardening," Jensen provided advice on planting design for large-scale landscapes.[18] Prior to this he had published under the Americanized byline of "James Jensen." With this article he returned to his given name, Jens Jensen. Reclaiming his Danish origins suggests that he had finally established his true identity in his new home in America's Middle West.

The papers he wrote at this time also introduced many of the basic ideas that would become fundamental to his lifetime work on regionally based design criteria: the role of public parks in alleviating overcrowding; the therapeutic benefits resulting from being surrounded by living plants; the need for promoting democratic institutions and environments; and criticism of prevailing landscaping techniques and attitudes.

His writing also began expressing his growing knowledge of landscape ecology gained from his extensive fieldwork and his friendship with University of Chicago Professor Henry Chandler Cowles, one of the founders of North American ecology. Jensen's development into a standard bearer for the Prairie School–style in landscape architecture was, in part, an outgrowth of his association with Cowles. Together they explored the Indiana sand dunes on club outings organized in Chicago. By then Cowles had written his seminal work "The Ecological Relations of the Vegetation on the Sand Dunes of Lake Michigan."[19] In his article "The Advance of Ecology," Ervin Zube, a prominent researcher in landscape architecture, noted that the friendship of Cowles and Jensen was an important collaboration for it served to introduce scientific ecology to the profession of landscape architecture at the beginning of the twentieth century.[20] During this crucial transformation, Jensen, a graduate of an agricultural school in Denmark, began to think less like a German-trained horticulturalist (he had studied the formal gardens of Berlin while serving his required military term) and more like an American ecologist.

While Jensen undoubtedly considered himself an artist, his published work contains a number of scientific papers on landscape ecology topics. His knowledge of botany is indicated in his two-part essay "Soil Conditions and Tree Growth around Lake Michigan," published in 1904.[21] In these articles he expressed his detailed knowledge about the geographic range of tree species. Jensen's design work after publishing these essays indicates an increasing awareness of the importance of using indigenous species for local soil and climatic conditions and portrays his growing understanding of ecology.

Jensen saw landscape architecture as the art form most capable of capturing and symbolizing the spirit of the prairie region. In "Hawthorns in the Landscape," he made his first attempt to describe his feelings about the Midwest's indigenous landscapes.[22] His graceful prose extolled the virtues of native plants such as the hawthorn, which he later used as a professional logo. Jensen was particularly fond of this tree, stating in the article that "[t]heir low spreading heads, their almost horizontal branches, melt into the broad, level stretches and teach us a lesson in the composition of landscape. . . . No June bride was ever more beautifully adorned than the meadows wreathed with the white blossoms of the hawthorn."[23] The crabapple, wild plum, dogwood, goldenrod, maple, and oak were also among his favorites. He adopted this short list of plants as part of his palette for creating native landscape designs and expressed his fondness for them over and over as his career progressed. The essay articulates ideas Jensen incorporated after designing the American Garden in Union Park—his first project to incorporate native plants.

Yet in the two years following his ecological papers, Jensen still retained ornamental gardening interests. His two articles for *Garden Magazine*, a national publication edited by fellow Prairie-style advocate Wilhelm Miller, offered practical advice on bulb beds and edging plants (mostly exotics).[24] (These are not included in this book.) They caution against portraying Jensen as a sudden convert to a pure native-plant design philosophy. Yet they show Jensen's interest in publishing for a wider national audience, which helped him establish a reputation beyond the Chicago region.

Subsequently, Jensen's 1906 article "Landscape Art—An Inspiration from the Western Plains" makes it clear that he attempted to take his "inspiration" from the native landscape. Rather than conceiving his work as merely an ecosystem restoration, Jensen believed the elements of nature were to be symbolic features of an artistic expression.[25] This artistic attitude is also evident in Jensen's writing style, which conveyed exuberance for his subject, poetic phrasing, and a metaphorical comparison between landscape architecture and the other fine arts, with preference given to landscape art's similarity to music composition. By this time Jensen's essays reflected his dual expertise in both art and basic ecology. This somewhat unusual relationship between art and science remains a distinguishing characteristic of the field of landscape architecture.

■ ■ ■

Following park reform efforts in Chicago politics, Jensen was rehired in 1905 as superintendent and landscape architect of the West Park System. In this capacity he took great pride in his work at Garfield Park, and under his supervision the Garfield Park conservatory—considered innovative because Jensen wanted it to fit into the midwestern landscape by having it resemble the outlines of a haystack—was built. By this time Chicago was alive with optimism, experiencing an era of intellectual and social creativity. It was embracing the advent of American ecology, the Prairie School of architecture with Louis Sullivan and Frank Lloyd Wright, the Chicago School in human ecology with Robert Park and Ernest Burgess, and the development of a Middle Western ethos that found expression in the poetry of Carl Sandburg and Vachel Lindsay. In this environment Jensen continued working on the estates of some of Chicago's most prominent citizens. This was often done in collaboration with some of the city's renowned architects, including Sullivan and Wright.

In 1908, as a member of Chicago's prestigious City Club, Jensen commented on the desperate need for parks on the city's West Side at the group's meetings focused on Chicago's playgrounds and park centers. As an employee of the West Park System, he was aware of the acute overcrowding in west Chicago and the lack of open, green space for its citizens. He pointed out that the West Parks had been given only enough money and authority to create just three small parks to serve as neighborhood centers. "Just think, only three for 1,000,000 people, and every one extremely small at that," he wrote.[26] He noted that wealthier parts of Chicago had much better facilities, and he worried about the effect of neglecting the West Side, stating, "It is better to build parks than to produce penitentiaries and insane asylums."[27]

He also penned five articles in 1908 and 1909 that focused on the design and significance of garden art and other key landscape details.[28] His "Some Gardens of the Middle West," published in the *Architectural Review* was especially effective in explaining his ideas about these features in an outdoor setting.[29]

In 1910 Jensen published "Improving a Small Country Place," his longest and most widely distributed article up to that time.[30] It was addressed to "the man whose means are limited." In it he revealed many of his "basic principles of landscape gardening." The piece is noteworthy not only for its design insights; it also conveys Jensen's egalitarian spirit, since his advice was intended for an owner of a parcel of land smaller than the typical aristocratic estate of the time. Reprinted into pamphlet form by the Illinois Outdoor Improvement Association, it sold for 10 cents and featured the request to "read and circulate" on its cover, which suggests Jensen's interest in reaching the middle class with landscaping advice. Unlike other landscape architects of the period, Jensen was not content to create works of art for society's elite. Instead, Jensen was concerned with improving the American environment in general and thereby improving its people and culture.

In the period between 1911 and 1916 Jensen began responding to the emerging city planning movement in America. He was opposed to the Neoclassical City Beautiful movement, the epitome of which was found in the buildings at the 1893 World's Columbian Exposition in Chicago. Jensen and the great Prairie School architect Louis Sullivan felt betrayed by European Beaux-Arts mimicry on view at the fairgrounds and that helped lay the foundation of a new city planning movement. The famous Burnham plan for Chicago, with its wide boulevards and monumental civic buildings, was anathema to Jensen's belief that America and the Middle West needed to develop their own architectural identities. As chairman of the Chicago City Club's city planning committee, Jensen wrote "Regulating City Building" in 1911. It was critical of both the City Beautiful style and the authoritarian actions needed to implement its plans. He noted:

To build civic centers and magnificent boulevards, leaving the greatest part of the city in filth and squalor, is to tell an untruth, to put on a false front, which vitiates the whole atmosphere of the town. The formal show environment reacts upon the people: the spirit of being on parade, of striving always for superficialities, makes of them a city of spendthrifts desirous of a gay life. As a consequence, immorality, strife, and discontent grow. The formal show city is distinctly imperialistic. It is undemocratic and its tendencies are destructive to the morals of its people. The more formal in design the less democracy in its feeling and tendency.[31]

This passage reveals much about Jensen's overall political and design philosophy. The last line was especially pertinent regarding his preference for the natural over the formal features in design. As an immigrant who had experienced the authoritarianism of Prussian occupation in Denmark, he was a true believer in the democratic ideals of the United States.

Jensen's criticism of city planning went beyond its design of civic spaces and buildings to its basic disregard for the natural setting of most American cities. As he did with his landscape designs, Jensen stressed the importance of designing cities for local conditions to give them their individuality.

Jensen's development from 1902 to 1918 indicates a growing confidence in and clarification of his beliefs. The scale of his work also increased from park floral beds to large estates, entire towns, and extensive conservation reserves. Articles, speeches, and planning reports from these crucial years reveal his progression from working on individual parks to making plans for entire park systems, such as one for Racine, Wisconsin. His Riverside Park report for New York City pitted his philosophy of park development against the actions of railroad engineers, who planned to cut a right-of-way through the Hudson Valley waterfront.[32] (Neither park plan is included herein.) The report expresses Jensen's concern for conservation of the natural environment, which in later years would grow into larger-scale conservation efforts. But, again, like his other conservation and park efforts, Jensen's argument for the preservation of Riverside Park was motivated by his belief "that the various influences of the out-of-doors are as essential to the full development of the intelligent human being as are other educational means."[33] This statement expressed Jensen's interest in education and foreshadows the founding of his version of a folk school in Wisconsin's Door County.

In 1917, following his Riverside Park report, Jensen made quick use of the new legislation creating the National Park Service by fighting to conserve his beloved

Indiana sand dunes at the southern tip of Lake Michigan. Jensen was a friend of the park service's first director, Chicago industrialist Stephen Mather. Both were members of the Friends of Our Native Landscape and the Prairie Club; the latter group made frequent excursions to significant Chicago-area landscapes, including the dunes. Jensen's testimony during the public hearing on a proposal to create a Sand Dunes National Park was a beautiful expression of his emotional and spiritual connection with this unique place. He began his testimony by pleading the need of Chicagoans—"us poor prairie folks"—to have the experience of topographic variation.[34] More so than in his previous published essays, Jensen's feelings seemed to highlight the contents of the Park Service report. Applause and laughter are recorded in the transcript as Jensen attempted to share his aesthetic experiences in the "dune country" with the audience and park commission. His oratory was personal, poetic, and infused with a spiritual argument for the conservation of the dunes that characterized his mysticism regarding the qualities and effects of landscapes. Perhaps the most interesting window into Jensen's thoughts is the passage where he stated:

> Now, I am not going to talk about recreational needs. I understand it has been assigned to me to talk about the trees. I do not like to be assigned to anything. [Laughter.] There are others who will tell you all about the trees. . . . What I want to impress on your minds is the beauty and grandeur of this dune country.[35]

Rather than speak on the obvious professional topics for a landscape architect—recreation and trees—Jensen insisted that the commission consider the needs of city dwellers to "revive their souls in the outglow of beauty from the dunes."[36]

As in his report on Riverside Park, Jensen's testimony regarding the sand dunes is representative of his evolution into a social critic. He understood that decisions about the environment reflected inherent values, especially those of society's elite. In the Riverside report he had complained about the lack of thought given to New York City's aesthetic improvement, writing, "Commerce is as important as art, that we know; but to sacrifice art for commerce is to sacrifice life itself."[37] Jensen was equally blunt with his sand dunes remarks, arguing:

> That it would be a sad thing, indeed, for this great Central West if this wonderful dune country should be taken away from us and on it built cities like Gary, Indiana Harbor, and others. It would show us to be in fact what we often are accused of being—a people who only have dollars for eyes.[38]

Having started as a street sweeper with the West Park System, Jensen was able to improve his station in life while still keeping the needs of working people foremost in his mind. In concert with the ideals of the Progressive movement popular between 1890 and 1920, he advocated for the urban working class. In his letter to the National Park Service regarding Sand Dunes National Park he wrote:

> No one has more need of an intimate acquaintance with out-of-door life and the always changing charms of nature than those who grind away their lives in our mills, our factories, our shops, and our stores. The man in the factory turning out the same kind of work day after day during his entire lifetime needs something as a balance, something that will make his work more endurable, more cheerful, something that will broaden his vision and save him or his descendants from the destruction sure to follow the endless grind of his daily life. The people of the mills, the shops, and the stores are the backbone of the great cities. They are the producers of wealth and the human species.[39]

■ ■ ■

From 1916 to 1918 Jensen created what he considered his most successful park design: Columbus Park in Chicago. It is a masterpiece expressing his design philosophy of utilizing native landscapes to educate and relieve the stress of overcrowded and over-worked city residents of Chicago's West Side. Designed in 1917, Columbus Park was Jensen's only opportunity to work on a new and undeveloped Chicago landscape rather than an existing city park.

As a member of the Chicago Geographical Society, Jensen was no doubt aware of the group's published articles on surveys of the extent of the area's ancient lakeshore. Just as he used his knowledge of ecology for native plantings, he also relied on his keen eye for geographic and topographic variations to evoke a local sense of place. His prairie river lagoon in Columbus Park was designed to follow the outline of an ancient beach form and native aquatic plants were utilized in the river to symbolize an Illinois riverway.

Justifiably proud of his Columbus Park creation, Jensen wrote several articles about it and included the park's plan in *Siftings*. His first written comments about it were in the *Forty-Ninth Annual Report of the West Chicago Park Commissioners* for 1917.[40] It was a straightforward description of the design and not as illuminating as subsequent articles in which he mentioned the park; those were written more than ten years after Columbus Park was completed and at a time when his greatest design work was behind him. His writing by that time had become retrospective, and he was able to trace the progress of his development as an artist. He would discuss his search for a Middle Western landscape aesthetic, from his discovery of the beauty of the crabapple and hawthorn in the 1880s and his experiments with native trees and "stratified rock" formations on a private estate in the 1890s to his work on Humboldt and Garfield Parks and his creation of Columbus Park.[41] Only at the latter was he satisfied that he had eliminated "notes of discord," in his design, stating, "Complete harmony is made possible only by keeping the composition pure; by that is meant the use of native plants only."[42] Both Jensen and fellow Prairie-style landscape architect O. C. Simonds became progressively purer in their use of native plants as they grew older and more experienced.

Jensen's genius as a landscape architect may have come from his ability to weave together the various and sometimes disparate strands of the profession, including the physical sciences of horticulture, ecology, and geology; the human-centered sciences of environmental psychology and human ecology; and even the humanities and the high arts of painting, sculpture, literature, and music. His Columbus Park design was emblematic of aspects of all these disciplines. "No park development worth speaking of has been done since the creation of Columbus Park," he wrote.[43]

The former street sweeper and park superintendent finished his employment at the West Park System as consulting landscape architect, creating a plan for expanding the park system. Jensen worked on the plan from initial surveys in 1917 and 1918 to its release in 1920. Published in book form, the impressive plan included attractive illustrations, elaborate typography, a generous number of photographs (which Jensen complained were difficult to shoot due to smoke from the city), colorful maps of metropolitan Chicago, and bird's-eye views of proposed park expansion areas.[44] His use of geographical determinants, such as greenways along the Chicago and Des Plaines Rivers and ancient beach forms, set a precedent for ecological planning methodologies developed by prominent landscape architects such as Ian McHarg and Philip H. Lewis Jr. in the second half of the twentieth century.

Jensen's *A Greater West Park System* report was in fact more than a plan for parks; it was a detailed expression for expanding the metropolis in an orderly manner around greenway (or "prairie drive") boulevards, large metropolitan parks, and con-servation reserves along the rivers. In place of the shacks, mud streets, and land-scapes ravaged by haphazard industrial development, he proposed a well-designed city with "neighborhood centers" and a "belt of parks, playgrounds, community kitchen gardens and community farms."[45]

The plan also contained one of Jensen's best representations of ideals for city design and urban life. His plan for a prairie drive west of Columbus Park incorporated mixed-use development featuring houses interspersed with apartment buildings and stores. The buildings faced the street, and their backyards opened to large "meadow" areas that provided greenery along a prairie drive. This scheme reflected his concern about overcrowding in Chicago's West Side, yet contrasted sharply with Frederick Law Olmsted's suburban ideas for a low-density and exclusively residential development—"Riverside"—designed in 1869 as an escape from Chicago. While Olmsted's design primarily stressed private space on private estates, Jensen's prairie drive plan accentuated public open spaces with pedestrian paths leading to residential and commercial structures. His vision was to take the drab and monotonous urbanized grid and make it green with living plants and alive with social activity in an environment that would foster happy citizens and democratic sentiments.

Realizing that not all of the city could be laid out again, Jensen offered a "suggestion as to how a quarter section of Chicago, overlaying the ordinary checker-board plan, might become attractive."[46] The key to this redesign was his notion of neighborhood centers that brought together school buildings and playgrounds in a public green or commons. These neighborhood centers would also contain school gardens for children, council rings for stories and debate, a players' hill for dramatic productions, and an old folks' corner. His hope was that these centers would provide a place where citizens young and old could freely associate. The design also reflected his belief in generous sites for municipal kitchen gardens. Having worked for the West Park System most of his adult life, Jensen understood the limitations of parks for curing social ills. Instead, he believed citizens needed more than an aesthetic experience, suggesting that one's relationship to the earth should be more intimate—like that of the gardener. He stated: "Parks and playgrounds offer a place for wholesome sport and social pleasure, and a place of rest and quiet from the noisy street. This, however, is only one phase of city building. To surround each home with a garden must be the final solution of urban life."[47]

Jensen was both a landscape architect and a conservationist. Publication of *A Greater West Park System* might be regarded as the turning point when his work and interest shifted from creating new environments to conserving vestiges of the natural world. While he continued to design private estates throughout the 1920s, his civic concerns turned from urban parks to preserving larger landscapes.

Another important theme introduced in Jensen's writings at this time is that of landscape appreciation. Published in 1920 and 1921 respectively, "I Like Our Prairie Landscape" and "Wisconsin Beautiful" are impressionistic essays in which he attempted to share his aesthetic experiences of landscapes.[48] As he did in his oratory on the Indiana dunes, Jensen's writing in these pieces revealed his emotional reaction to the vibrant colors and textures of these landscapes. Jensen understood native landscapes to be the work of ecological processes over the ages and claimed that "landscape gardening is the one art that is dependent upon soil and climatic conditions."[49]

Jensen's early essays dealing with conservation were a mixture of wonder and lament; in them he was both art critic and defender of the natural environment. After arriving in Chicago in 1885, he had witnessed the taming of the midwestern landscape: the plowing of the last of the great prairie, the clear-cutting of the northern forest, and the never-ending urban expansion. Jensen feared the onslaught of mono-culture, industrialization, and commercialization.

Especially vexing was the destruction of natural wonders by profit seekers. In "Wisconsin Beautiful" Jensen described his only visit, in the 1890s, to the "Dalles" of the Wisconsin River, which then had "one of their greatest charms, the roaring of the waters through the narrows."[50] However, he complained, "I have never visited the Dalles since, and I do not expect to be there again, because their greatest charm has been destroyed by commercial greed." (The despoilment he references resulted from extensive commercial development and the construction of a dam, which ruined portions of the river's charm.) The article is also significant because it includes a description of his first journey to Door County, Wisconsin: "we turned down the cliffs at Fish Creek far above the jagged shore line now illuminated by the afterglow of the setting sun and below the indigo blue waters of Green Bay. What I saw on that first visit drew me close to Door County."[51]

■ ■ ■

By 1920 Jensen's work for the West Park System was completed. At this point he began making a break with Chicago and city life. The entry of the United States into World War I had had a sobering effect on the Chicago School (of which Jensen was a member) and the cultural movement it represented. Its philosophy of the Middle West's own cultural expression seemed at odds with technological innovations in high-speed transport, instant communications, and the new era of mass media centered in New York. Jensen started living part of each year in a wooded area of northern Door County, leaving behind the role of civic activist and becoming a prophetic voice speaking and writing on conservation matters. By the turn of the century Jensen had become a key advocate for preserving a system of forest reserves around Chicago. Working with plant ecologist Henry Chandler Cowles, architect Dwight Perkins, and others, he contributed to the movement for state action to conserve a system of preserves along the Des Plaines River, from Lake Michigan on the north to Calumet Lake on the south.

Realizing the necessity of promoting conservation of unique ecosystems to government officials and the public alike, Jensen, along with several like-minded individuals, founded the Friends of Our Native Landscape in 1913. The group, which included some of Chicago's most influential citizens, became the organizational tool Jensen needed to call attention to opportunities for conservation and thereby create an atmosphere conducive to new public policies. The group's publications were an important vehicle for informing the public about conservation issues. In one such publication Jensen stated his desire to "eventually make our State [Illinois] one great park where the primitive America will vie in interest and beauty with the rural country."[52] Also of interest in these essays is Jensen's fascination with Native American culture and the preservation of reminders of early pioneer history.

In 1923 Jensen began writing about his work and philosophy for a German gardening magazine, publishing "Die Landschaftsgäertnerei—eine Kunst" ("Landscape Gardening—An Art") in *Gartenschöenheit*.[53] In this piece he eloquently expressed some of his basic philosophical views about respecting the indigenous qualities of a landscape and the characteristics of the gardens of ordinary Americans. "We cannot attain a healthy and normal civilization without a certain influence from the original, the prehistoric soil, in which we are all rooted which is a part of our selves and always should remain so," he stated.[54]

In the 1920s, at the urging of Simonds, Jensen, and others, the use of native species was looked upon with greater fervor. While Jensen was critical of the emerging automobile culture, he saw roadsides as an opportunity for using native plants. In "Roadside Planting,"[55] one of only two articles he contributed to *Landscape Architecture*, a publication of the American Society of Landscape Architects (ASLA), he argued against lining highways with rows of trees in a manner similar to the "stately avenues of monarchies."[56] In this piece Jensen combined aesthetic concerns with an appeal to American democratic ideals—a favorite rhetorical device for Jensen. A striking feature of his style of persuasion was his return to a personal experience with a landscape in essay after essay.

In his second article for *Landscape Architecture*, "Novelty Versus Nature," Jensen described changes to the woodland around his Ravinia, Illinois, studio in terms similar to an earlier essay, "Marring the Landscape."[57] He was especially angered by what he considered the stupidity of cutting down mature trees to introduce new nursery stock.

Unlike most ASLA members, Jensen was not a graduate of a university curriculum in landscape architecture. (The Harvard program, established in 1900, was the first, and arguably remains the preeminent one in the United States.) Nevertheless Jensen was elected to membership in the organization in 1923 and welcomed the group at its annual meeting in Chicago in 1926. But he soon became disenchanted with the ASLA and resigned the following year. It is generally surmised that his dislike of the organization stemmed from the formal and exotic landscape design styles favored by many of its members. He would later refer to them as "high priests," or "the white collar" group.[58]

■ ■ ■

In 1925 Jensen's second German article "Amerikanische Gartengedanken" ("American Garden Thoughts") was published in *Gartenschöenheit*.[59] In it he described his views about some fundamental characteristics of "the typical garden of the majority in the United States." He mentioned their "openness and freedom," stating "this freedom will be expressed in our gardens despite the constant introduction of European ideas."[60]

The following year Jensen wrote "The Park Policy" section for the Friends of Our Native Landscape's report, *A Park and Forest Policy for Illinois*.[61] In this comprehensive proposal he recommended specific areas greater "than one thousand acres in area" for state parks. He cautioned that they "should be held as free from man-made reminders as is possible. They should not have dance pavilions or merry-go-rounds. These things belong in the city and the village; they are out of place in reservations that are dedicated to nature's beauty."[62]

Continuing to expound on his basic philosophy, in 1927 he published "Nature the Source," in the *Vista*, the annual publication of the University of Illinois's University Landscape Architects' Society.[63] Again, he insisted on a holistic conception of the relationship between humans and landscapes, neither reducing the environment to the level of a utilitarian natural resource to be exploited nor elevating the "primitive wilderness" to a status degraded by the presence of human beings. "Man is an insepa-rable part of the whole creation—the sea, the mountains, the forest, the streams, the hills, the valleys and its wild life," he wrote.[64] He concluded by relating some of his childhood recollections, including his intellectual development, and the role of the Danish landscape and its folk schools in creating in him a "new feeling, a new love for native soil."

That spring Jensen visited Madison, Wisconsin, to speak before the state legisla-ture and give an illustrated lecture at the University of Wisconsin. He called the talk "Landscape Appreciation," and it was subsequently published in *Wisconsin Horticulture*.[65] (The article is rarely cited by scholars since publication of this journal ceased in 1967.) In it Jensen wrote eloquently of how "the out-of-doors . . . has penetrated my soul and influenced my life." He again referred to the boyhood experiences in Denmark that "added to my vision and enriched my life."[66]

During the summer of 1927, he wrote the first of several articles for *Our Native Landscape*, an occasional publication of the Wisconsin Friends of Our Native Landscape chapter; it was published until 1935.[67] These small pamphlets included articles by many members of the group, including such prominent Wisconsinites as Zona Gale, Joseph Schafer, and C. B. Whitnall. Around this time Jensen also contributed an article on beech trees native to the Chicago region.[68] The in-depth understanding of ecology expressed in it indicated that Jensen could be ranked with some of the leading scientists of Illinois.

In 1930 Jensen wrote about Columbus Park in greater detail than ever before in "The Naturalistic Treatment in a Metropolitan Park," published in *American Landscape Architect*.[69] He described the conditions of its original prairie site and gave a detailed explanation of the rationale behind his plan. It was, he said, "as much an attempt to realize a complete interpretation of the native landscape of Illinois as anything which the author has done."

That year he also published "Natural Parks and Gardens" in the *Saturday Evening Post*.[70] This popular and widely circulated magazine offered Jensen the largest audience of his publishing career. With the byline of "Jens Jensen As Told to Ragna B. Eskil," it was his first collaboration with another writer. Considering the content, biographical scope, layout, and photos likely taken by Jensen, it is one of his finest publications.

During the early 1930s Jensen continued his conservation battles but did little publishing except for a few brief articles and a report on roadside planting and development that he wrote with several members of the Friends of Our Native Landscape.[71] Also, his keynote address, "Conservation in the Regional Plan," was included in the 1934 report from the organization's conference on state and regional planning.[72]

Later that year his wife, Anna Marie, passed away and several months later Kenneth Jensen Wheeler, Jensen's talented grandson and the heir apparent to his practice, died. In addition to these personal tragedies Jensen had become increasingly disillusioned with cities and city life. Thus, he closed his studio at Ravinia and moved to rural Ellison Bay in Door County, Wisconsin, to realize his lifelong dream of starting what he called a "school of the soil." His starting this school, The Clearing, can be seen as mirroring the reasons for the creation of folk schools in Denmark after German occupation of three of its provinces in 1864. Jensen wished to teach young people to appreciate their own native landscapes and embrace indigenous traditions rather than simply accepting cultural expressions from outside the region. His hope was that in America's Middle West a new place-bound culture would emerge. To him, this dream seemed unfulfilled, as Chicago became increasingly tied to the national and international scene. Several unpublished and undated typewritten versions of Jensen's goals for The Clearing exist, including the mid-1930s "A Program for School of the Soil."[73] However, his ideas would be scaled back in subsequent years primarily because of financial difficulties resulting from the Great Depression.

In 1937 Jensen wrote three more articles for German gardening magazines, including "Die 'Lichtung'" ("The 'Clearing'"), which describes the buildings and surrounding landscape of his new home.[74] Of interest is his mention of the nonnative plants he used: "My plantings around the log cabin are in harmony with the woodland, mostly native species with the exception of a few special plants for the immigrant and a few friendly greetings from Illinois."[75]

By this time the National Socialist Party was in control of all aspects of German cultural expression, including the content of magazines. They found Jensen's philosophy of using native plants and appreciation of native landscapes consistent with their propaganda themes of "Fatherland" and the superiority of Germanic traditions rooted in their native soil. However, Jensen's views on this did not support the racial policies of the Nazis. His preference for native plants and landscapes was primarily part of his approach to design; apparently he had not accepted the xenophobia nascent in such a philosophy. Back in 1924 his friend Jane Addams had asked him to address the Women's International League for Peace and Freedom's Summer School at the Fine Arts Building in Chicago. The theme for the gathering was "The Human Factors in Internationalism." Jensen's speech, "The Nordic's Contribution to America," was important because he discussed some of his views against xenophobia and restricting immigration. He said:

> *I believe in everybody coming to America. I do not believe in any restriction of the yellow races or black races or any other races. . . . Either you must be so selfish that you bring in yourself only, or you must admit everybody, and I am for everybody.*[76]

The charge that Jensen's beliefs were aligned with those of the Nazis was also refuted in an extensive article, "Jens Jensen, Native Plants, and the Concept of Nordic Superiority," published in 1999.[77]

Consistent with his beliefs, Jensen urged his fellow New World immigrants to do exactly what the Nazis feared: let the landscape of America inspire a new culture and also the appreciation of the local cultures that existed before the arrival of Europeans. He had great respect for Native Americans and fought to preserve remaining vestiges of their culture.

In 1938 Jensen was invited to give a paper at the International Horticultural Conference in Berlin. He was unable to attend and his friend Franz Aust, professor of landscape architecture at the University of Wisconsin, read the paper in his stead. In it Jensen reflected on the American environment and explained the philosophy behind his work to create landscapes that reflected its identity.

During the 1930s and 1940s, Jensen wrote a flurry of letters and guest editorials for the *Chicago Daily News*, the *Chicago Tribune*, the *Milwaukee Journal*, and the *Door County Advocate*. In 1936 he met William T. Evjue, editor of Madison's *Capital Times*, who vacationed in Door County each summer. The two men became good friends and Evjue sometimes wrote editorials on Jensen's views about conservation. In 1940 Jensen began contributing a frequent column featured on the newspaper's editorial page. For nearly a decade he wrote on such topics as his support for the new Ridges Sanctuary in Baileys Harbor; his pleas to designate a state park at the majestic sand dunes of Whitefish Bay; the value of wildlife; his appreciation for roadside beauty; his criticism of park and game management policies; his views about democracy; the need for civilization to be "rooted in the soil"; and a variety of other topics he felt necessary to speak out about. He also often gave talks to civic groups, universities, garden clubs, and other organizations. By this time his fiery conservation activism was receiving considerable publicity in the press.

■ ■ ■

Jensen's attitude as expressed in his writings cannot be easily simplified; it was complex and somewhat contradictory. At times he seems a man out-of-place—still missing Denmark but finding America more colorful and wild. While it is clear he wanted America to develop its own cultural expression, Jensen personally enjoyed the works of European masters in literature, art, and music. His landscape design style was predicated on respecting an area's sense of place, as well as using indigenous plants and local building materials. His political and religious ideals were best conveyed in his writing, particularly the guest editorials he wrote for newspapers in Chicago and Madison during the 1930s and 1940s.

Jens Jensen died in 1951 at the age of ninety-one. During his long and productive career, he exemplified integrity but could also be fiery, controversial, and contradictory. But above all he was a visionary who designed landscapes of delight, fought to conserve important natural environments, and served as a social advocate who worked tirelessly to establish better living conditions for all. In many respects his work and dreams live on today at projects he designed, especially his beloved school, The Clearing, which, thanks to his dedicated successors, particularly his longtime secretary Mertha Fulkerson, remains a special place for discovering the experience with nature he wanted all Americans to have.

Jensen at The Clearing, mid-1930s

Courtesy of The Clearing

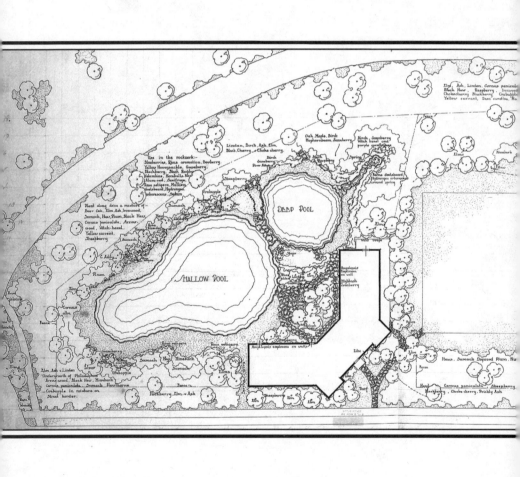

WRITINGS
INSPIRED BY
NATURE

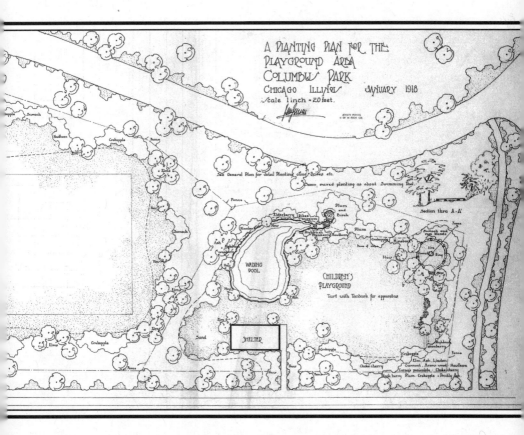

A PLANTING PLAN FOR THE
PLAYGROUND AREA
COLUMBUS PARK
CHICAGO ILLINOIS   JANUARY 1918
Scale 1 inch = 20 feet.

See General Plan for detail Planting along Drives etc.

Section thru A-A'

WADING
POOL

CHILDREN'S
PLAYGROUND
Turf with Tanbark for apparatus

SHELTER

EXTERMINATION OF THE OAK AT LAKE GENEVA, WISCONSIN

The Forester, March 1901

The threatened destruction of the beautiful forest lands around the well known summer resort, Lake Geneva, Wisconsin, has become an important question to those owning houses, and passing the summer months at this place. In my profession as landscape architect, the opportunity offered itself to make a careful study of those causes destroying the great oaks in wholesale fashion.

The contour of the land is rolling, sometimes changing into abrupt grades towards the Lake or natural water courses. Gravel or gravelly soil prevails on the higher lands. On lower lands the gravel is covered by layers, varying in thickness, of hard pan in some instances, and of a gravelly clay containing some vegetable matter in others. Seemingly these layers have been washed down from the higher lands. The low lands along the natural water courses consist of black loam or decayed vegetable matter that, in some instances, becomes boggy; but this is of no special interest here, as it is on the gravel or clay lands that the oak has made its home. Close observation shows that trees growing on the "hard-pan" lands have suffered more than those on more porous grounds, and especially on lands turned into private parks, whether of gravel or clay substance.

Besides the oak, the Ironwood—(*Carpinus betula*) is gradually becoming extinct. The affliction is general; young and old are alike effected. Such varieties, or species as the Scarlet Oak (*Q. coccinea*), the White Oak (*Q. alba*), the Red Oak (*Q. rubra*), suffer most; whereas the Bur-Oak or Mossycup Oak (*Q. macrocarpa*), holds its own. The Pin Oak (*Q. palustris*) and several other species are not found in sufficient numbers in this district to permit satisfactory observation.

During the latter part of July and the first part of August last trees in supposedly healthy condition suddenly withered as if struck by blight. In some instances this withering of the leaves was confined to certain limbs or branchlets only. Supposing that this sudden attack was caused by a fungus of some kind, I sent several leaves to Professor Bryon H. Halstead for examination. The reply was: "The oak leaves you send show some trouble but not so clearly that the diagnosis is satisfactory"; and he further suggested that the trouble might be at the roots, due to some change that lessened the subterranean water supply. Upon this suggestion several roots were sent; but neither in this instance could there be found any indication of the trouble prevalent. This satisfied me that fungus had nothing, or very little, to do with the extermination of the Oak; but that Professor Halstead's suggestion as to lack of water supply was correct, even if the roots did not indicate it.

The cause which led to this wholesale dying out is undoubtedly not of recent date; and to get at the root of the trouble it would be necessary to turn back for almost a decade.

The drouths of 1893, 94, and '95 are still fresh in the memory of every one engaged in agriculture or horticulture; the drouth being quite general over the country. Losses were great in both industries, especially on higher levels or near large cities where artificial sewerage assisted in the work of destruction. During those three years the earth dried out to a considerable depth. Then I noticed by digging a sewer that at a depth of ten feet or more the ditch was perfectly dry; when under ordinary conditions water could be found at a depth of three or four feet. Was it possible for trees to obtain sufficient moisture under such conditions? Assuredly not. And here we may look for the starting point of those causes destroying the oak forest at Lake Geneva and other points.

The prevalence of dead trees on the "hard pan" lands, previously mentioned, is attributed to the fact that after these lands got thoroughly dry, the oaks could not absorb sustenance from the ground as in the more porous clay or gravelly lands. Consequently little or no water was conveyed to the roots of the already dying trees. We must also remember the rolling topography of the land, which gives little chance for the absorption of heavy rains and is especially lacking in those agencies that assist in holding water. Conditions of this sort were more prevalent on the so-called "improved" lands, where such beneficent agencies as undergrowth, in the shape of shrubbery or herbaceous perennials, and even the grass, had been cut off close to the ground. The outcome has been a larger amount of dead timber. Three years of drouth had dried out the soil to a considerable depth and very few roots were able to transmit moisture to the trees, which, cut off from their water supply, commenced to die. The trouble was first visible in the dead tops; but to the close observer the majority of trees suffered, and the weak growth produced gave assurance of the trouble.

The deadly attack on the sturdy oak had not yet reached its limit. The climax came with the severe winter of 1898–99—not only a winter known for its extreme low temperature, but one that will long be remembered for its scant fall of snow. The absence of snow removed that protection which nature so wisely provides, and thus enabled the frost to penetrate the ground to an unusual depth. Here again the barren "cultivated" slopes suffered the most. The action of this severe winter on tree growth was in many instances identical with that of the great drouths of previous years.

Apparently the trees are inactive during the winter months, and to some extent this is so. As an illustration we may compare this natural rest of trees with the winter sleep of animals and, like the latter, the trees need nourishment to sustain life. Thus the trees require a certain amount of water. A certain amount of evaporation is going on during the winter months, increasing in sunny weather and especially during the early spring. This evaporation becomes greater in trees retaining their foliage all winter, as, for instance, the evergreens; and one, therefore, often notices that those killed are badly damaged (browned) during the warm spring weather when the ground still remains frozen. When we talk about hardy trees getting "winter-killed" it does not mean a freezing to death through the structural tissues, but a disturbance in these parts caused by the impossibility of obtaining water through the solidly frozen, ground-enclosed roots, and partly through an uneven swelling and contraction of the wood, produced by excessive cold weather and sudden thawing. The latter can be noticed by the vertical splitting of the trunk, or loosening of the bark, and most often seen on short-grained or not over-hardy trees.

The causes that lead to the killing of soft woods or tender trees and shrubs are entirely different, and do not belong in this article. In most instances where a tree has been "winter killed" it will shoot up again from the roots showing that the latter do not suffer from severe frosts; and this again stands to show why Professor Halstead was unable to detect any trouble in the roots sent for examination.

Three years of drouth had left the trees that survived in a weak condition, and these were followed by an unusually cold and snowless winter, during which frost in exposed sections was carried down to such great depths that every root was embedded in a solid frozen mass. And this, continued till almost the first of May, a time when sap had commenced to flow and a sudden supply of water was in great demand, proved too much for the oak, and hundreds of trees succumbed to an unavoidable death.

Some may ask, why were not those Oaks standing alone in cultivated fields killed? They are more exposed and still seem to thrive far better than their sisters in the forest. Indeed they do. And why should they not? The plow and harrow have brought life into the soil. Water and heat are more easily absorbed and retained, and through cultivation close competitors have been removed and thus a larger area obtained to feed on.

Nature has wisely provided the forest with protection wherever it is needed and usually we find this the way of undergrowth. This canopy of vegetation served in several ways. First, it protects the ground from the hot sun during summer; thus cooling the surface and decreasing evaporation. During the winter it forms a warm blanket preserving the moisture which is increased by holding secure the falling leaves and drifting snow and preventing the frost from reaching to any great depth. These actions jointly encourage root-action near the surface in thoroughly decayed vegetable matter and enriched mother soil. And here again we may rightly assume that why trees are found to die out faster on "improved" lands is also because that "root-action" that through the natural protection of undergrowth had been encouraged near the surface, fell an easy victim to continued drouth, after the brush had been removed. The remedy for solving this, too often, perplexing problem, would be: protection, cultivation, and during extreme dry weather, artificial watering. If insufficient water supply was not the cause of extermination of the Oak, why did the larger trees, those demanding a larger supply of water commence to die out first? Why did trees growing under more favorable conditions in regard to obtaining water, after the dead tops had been removed, start out vigorously again? Why did trees on slopes or hilly, exposed grounds, suffer, and those on low and moist lands, not?

Now as to remedying this: First, protection. This may be accomplished either by inducing a luxuriant undergrowth to cover the ground in the way of shrubbery or herbaceous perennials, or by permitting the grass to grow long in the fall. This would hold the falling leaves and drifting snow, and form a warm blanket which would prevent the frost from going to a great depth. It would also decrease evaporation from the ground during the winter and summer, and add moisture and fertility, which in return encourages root-action near the surface.

Cultivation makes the soil porous, thus permitting the heat and moisture to penetrate it. Heat and moisture are necessary to the formation of such chemical combinations in the soil as supply food to the roots and bring renewed life to the trees.

Besides, as before mentioned, cultivation increases the retaining of moisture. Where the forest is thickly wooded a thinning out will give more light and nourishment to the remaining trees, and thereby induce better growth.

PLAN FOR HOSPITAL GROUNDS

Park and Cemetery, December 1901

To prepare plans for the gardens of a hospital designated to the treatment of consumptives is not an everyday occurrence. No suggestions were offered by the board of directors or the medical staff. That the patients would receive a large percentage of their treatment from outdoor exercise became at once apparent and perhaps the gardens would add greatly to the popularity of the hospital as an advertising medium.

The divided garden plot gave encouragement to produce two distinctly different designs, something that should not be overlooked in a place where every added attraction would prove of great benefit to the patient-visitor.

Thus one side has been laid out into a miniature park, with plenty of walks, pretty scenery, abundance of sunlight and sheltered to the north by evergreen plantation, which in return will have a healthy influence upon the sick, make the garden useful in bright winter weather, and give character to the winter landscape. In the other part a large lawn for kindred games, a flower garden and a maze or tangle of walks for exercise have been provided.

The buildings are situated in the best location possible, where the sun will be able to lend its health bringing rays to every room, leaving plots on each side for garden purposes in full view from the sick rooms.

The main entrance is one of some breadth, giving splendid view of the rather pretty building and the gardens to either side.

Just in front of the entrance to the building stands a statue of St. Ann on a slightly raised terrace.

The rear building—not hospital—has been well hidden by such trees as elms, lindens and soft maples, with an undergrowth of Philadelphus and high bush cranberry, and the front buildings relieved by climbers and a heavy planting of low growing shrubs. . . . The rear court is to be constructed of cement for cleanliness' sake, with sufficient room left along the walls of the building for climbing plants such as Ampelopsis Veitchii (cuspidata) and Engelmanni to soften and relieve the hard tones of this stony inclosure.

Native trees and shrubs with a sprinkling of Russian mulberry and Ailanthus glandulosa constitute the border plantations.

Those parts having evergreen plantations have been elevated from 4 to 7 feet over the present surface by the excavations from the lily ponds, the border of which runs from a long easy slope at the lower south side to an abrupt stony projection where the summer house is located.

Besides pine and spruce those elevated grounds are covered with birch, walnut, thorn, crab, Amelanchier, Juneberry, plum and alder.

The pond border is to be planted with alder, thorn, dogwood, Tamarix, Ribes, Viburnum, potentilla, Iris, Typhas, Sagittarias, rushes and grasses. Add to this the pond filled with water lilies and alive with goldfish, and perhaps no more interesting and beautiful spot could be created for either sick or healthy.

The spaces between the walks in the maze are to be planted with Ligustrum Ibota grown in natural form. Both flower garden and maze have been well hidden in the general view by heavy planting of trees and shrubs. For the latter the selection has been made to give effect to the sky line, and such trees as Lombard poplar, soft maple, European elm, wild cherry and white ash have been used with an undergrowth of choke cherry, Viburnum, sumach and buckthorn.

The northeast corner is devoted to fruit and vegetable garden, and on two sides bounded by avenues of cherry trees, one to be used as a service road, the other a promenade. White elms have been selected for street trees and a hedge of Ligustrum Ibota surrounds the entire grounds.

TOPIARY GARDENING

Park and Cemetery, July 1902

To those that have visited old English and Dutch gardens the "Topiary"—a garden of tree sculpture—is well known. But the majority of Americans are not familiar with this branch of gardening (?) of which a revival is being attempted in this country. The topiary consists of trees—mostly evergreen—pruned into imitation of anything that the eccentric owner's or gardener's fancy may desire, save the natural and noble beauty of the tree itself.

That this distortion of tree growth is as absurd as the reproduction of all kinds of plant sculpture—by some termed vaudeville gardening—through the aid of foliage plants, which became such a prominent feature of our parks a few years ago, must be evident to the true gardener and lover of nature's unquestioned beauty.

Whether it is the imitation of animated life or other objects by tree pruning or foliage plants, each work must be classed with the exhibitions of the dime museums, and from the frequenters of these institutions draw its admirers.

Topiary gardening reached its zenith in England in the sixteenth century and was supposed in those days to represent the highest skill to be attained in the noble profession of gardening. But with the higher intellect of succeeding centuries the profession threw off its yoke of barbarism and emerged into the gardenesque or naturalistic type of gardening, which, with a few minor changes, has remained until the present day. Is it not a fact that whereas sculpture and architecture never have been outclassed since the glorious days of Greece and Rome, gardening has steadily developed into an art demanding recognition and a place alongside that of other arts?

When Lord Byron said: "Man will build stately first and garden finely next, as if gardening was of a higher intellect," he spoke the truth. The gardens of early history—mere parts of the house—were not the creation of the gardener, but the architect, and in these so-called gardens stone and mortar played the most important role. First, after the profession of gardening had gained recognition, came the change to "real gardens," with trees, shrubbery and flowers. True types of the architect's products are still seen in Southern Europe to-day and especially in Italy in the so-called Italian gardens. Americans, charmed by this type of gardening, have been tempted to introduce them into this country, and deplorable indeed are the majority of those seen in the eastern states where they have gained a foothold. To create an Italian garden without the stately cypress is impossible. These gardens had their origin in southern countries and only there attain their true character. Admitting many beautiful points of the Italian garden, is there *one* in the topiary? The first represents art; does the latter? Topiary gardening has no claim on the profession as an art and its revival should be resented by every true gardener.

There always will be men with little intellect and plenty of money who, for the sake of popularity, will turn their gardens into museums of freaks where even the stalwart moonshiner would hesitate to pass through at the midnight hour.

PARKS AND POLITICS

Park and Cemetery, October 1902

The rapidly growing sentiment for creating parks for the congested population of this country needs support, and it may be truly said that its greatest achievements are still to come and therefore belong to the future. The era of park making appears upon the historical pages of a city when culture and refinement have penetrated the narrow spheres of commercialism, when the rude make-up of a city has been mastered, and accumulated wealth demands pleasure and comfort. Therefore, we find that the introduction of parks occurs at an epoch often injurious to the artistic layout of a great city, and which has to be overcome at an immense cost.

It is perhaps not always true that the motives creating public pleasure grounds are of that true and benevolent character uppermost in the hearts of those desirous for the welfare of their less fortunate fellowmen, but on the contrary come from a selfish desire to build parks and parkways as an incentive to increasing the value of their own land holdings. Whatever may be the original causes, however, the creation of parks by any city must be commended as the first step of municipal art out-of-doors, and a prime necessity for improving the health and morality of those that have to pass their lives in these congested spots.

Parks come into existence either through a general public demand inspired by men of higher intelligence, broad-minded, and with a love for Nature beautiful, or through the benevolence of some generous, loyal and public spirited citizen.

Nature and art are to go hand in hand crowned with the highest attainments possible by human conception, thereby adding to the prestige and good name of any city, and making life in these piles of brick and mortar worth living. Park making is a measure, by which, together with other great municipal undertakings, the intelligence of its citizens are judged.

In cities where the creation of parks has been largely due to public legislation, forethought and a careful perusal of the laws framed to convey, maintain and develop acquired lands into beautiful parks, have often been neglected and thus have permitted the first loophole for political misrule.

On the character and intelligence of the committee in charge depends the proper selection of lands best suitable, either on account of existing natural beauty, or convenience, and, in reference to population, justly located for park purposes, and the plans adopted for their improvement.

Thus it is readily seen that the very first and most important matter in park affairs is the selection of broad-minded, public-spirited men for the office of park trustees; men whose standing in the community is high, who take pleasure in putting in their spare hours inspecting the parks, who consider the office one of honor exclusively, and altogether are interested in art out-of-doors. With such men at the head of any park system, success is inevitable and is an honor to the city that has been so fortunate. Such men do not seek public office, but must be called upon to serve. But how is it possible to procure good men for park boards, when through inefficient laws, the acute eccentricities or questionable ambition of politicians, a governor or mayor may chop off their official heads without the least warning before the expiration of their term, whether their duties have been honestly and conscientiously discharged or not? How un-American such proceedings are, and yet nevertheless true; and I may ask what value can a park trustee render when not permitted to remain long enough in office to become familiar with his duties, and the same question may be asked concerning park employees. On the other hand, it is quite different with the political park trustee. He is apparent everywhere, pushing his claims for recognition to the very doors of the executive home, pointing to his victories on the political battlefield for which he demands office only to use it for the benefit of his agents. They in return for good services rendered, further the political ambition and selfish interest of their employer and political boss, to the continual detriment of the parks and its supporters. Wherever managements of this character are dominant, their influence is plainly visible.

Statuary of questionable art is accepted, or through an overzealous attempt to procure images of every one's idol, the quiet sylvan scenery of the park has been turned into an ancestral showplace, suggestive of certain of our cemeteries. Buildings of ugly and ill-fitting architecture obtrude upon pastoral meadows or are placed in spots inappropriate for any building. Innovations of all kinds including midways, where the "real thing" kneels down and loads or unloads its merry crew of sight-seers. Visionary tiger-hunts are indulged in from the safe back of a serviceable elephant, whose sudden appearance to the timid and unaware park visitor may cause hysterical convulsions. There are ice carnivals and dances—all for the good of the party. The advertisements of some merchant who is termed a "good fellow" are thrown upon the canvas at public concerts, running riot with the sacred melodies of Wagner. Floral designs of the most ridiculous and fantastic kinds find themselves perfectly at home in this great aggregation of show fixtures. The products of the conservatories are placed at the disposal of political friends, and free boating and fishing permits are scattered broadcast as bait for the unscrupulous voter. These are undeniable facts, misleading the uneducated as to what a park should be—a place of natural scenery and sylvan beauty brought to his very doorsteps and in which his weary body and overworked nerves can find the needed rest and comfort.

Shrewdness is one of the great traits of the professional politician; so we may often see that to avoid sharp criticism, the appointive power selects one man of "standing" to serve as a target on the park board; but he no sooner finds out his real mission than his resignation is placed at the disposal of the powers that be. Or, perhaps a superintendent of some qualification is selected to carry the misdeeds of the trustees on his shoulders. Has he any manhood at all, his services will be of short duration. Whether the park superintendent is a gardener of the political variety or a professional politician, whose sole duty is drawing his salary, is immaterial—the outcome is ultimately the same and perhaps in favor of the latter, whose attempt at disfiguring the park with inappropriate improvements is usually assured.

That the paying for a plan for proposed park lands, or its execution by a consulting landscape architect, ends the professional service, is folly. Who dare say that after the child is born, it is able to take care of itself? Upon its early education and association depends largely its usefulness in life. So it is with the caretaking of our parks. The development of such vegetation as forms the leading part in the construction of parks, is one of years, and its nursing needs the best of care obtainable. Continual destruction to the park scenery either from natural causes or through such agencies as polluted atmosphere, sewerage, insects, etc., characteristic of city environments, needs the watchfulness of the practical and artistic eye, if health and beauty shall dominate and the scenery be kept intact, or otherwise these agencies when permitted to proceed unrestrained, will soon have changed the once pretty landscape into ruin and desolation, and the original plan of the designer perverted to the discredit of the city that once adopted it. And how is this to be prevented when supervised by indifferent commissioners and impractical superintendents? The caretaker must be in thorough sympathy with the plans of the designer and to be so, he must be an artist himself. Parks are a necessity for the cultivation and preserving of a love for Nature. They are seats of learning for the average city-bred being, and their influence is plainly visible in shaded streets and pretty home surroundings. Parks are practical schools of horticulture, and the bone and sinew of municipal art out of doors. They are necessary for the self-preservation of those who by free will or through forced circumstances have made their homes in a large city.

And with all these facts—plain undeniable facts—they will be permitted to fall into decay through political mismanagement, a shameful spot upon the fair name of any city. Political supervision tends to destroy the beauty of our parks, promotes the carrying out of inartistic and useless improvements, depreciates real estate value, encourages immoral life and squanders public money; and they do not create for the city what originally was intended—a beautiful park, a lasting monument of nature and art, a practical demonstration of culture and refinement, to which the municipality may point with pride and honor.

That there do exist men with political ambition well qualified for the trustee-ship of our parks, is not denied, but these are above party politics and are able to resist the detrimental influence of the dominant ward-boss. It has been said that there are visible and invisible park boards—perhaps the invisible are the most dangerous.

Germany can perhaps be taken as a model in park management as it justly is in forestry. There every city or town has its gardener or garden-director, classed in rank with other heads of departments of municipal affairs.

How would it look if an advertisement appeared in one of our horticultural papers calling for a park superintendent for a certain city? This is of usual occurrence in Germany. An examination is held of the applicants, and the highest marked succeeds. The diploma of a college of horticulture, together with years of practical work in the different branches of gardening, are necessary qualifications for such positions. Unquestionably our schools of horticulture and landscape architecture should provide eligible men for the management of our parks, and a "Committee of Municipal Art," recommended by representative art associations and societies of architects, and civil engineers, named by the mayor, should appoint a commissioner of public parks.

The United States Department of Forestry has in its few years of existence shown the value of trained men in its service—let us hope that the municipalities will follow its steps.

MARRING THE LANDSCAPE

Park and Cemetery, 1902

The increased demand for planting trees and shrubbery on the city lot has called into activity everybody, from the basement excavator to the dealer in trees and shrubs, and the different types posing as landscapers can be seen at work everywhere in the fashionable residence district. And what a parody on landscape art! The barren lawns would do more credit to these imposing thoroughfares. Not only is the sense for artistic effect entirely lacking, but in many instances the ignorance of the proper size of trees and shrubs at mature age is one of the main causes of this deplorable planting. Or perhaps the desire has been to sell as many plants as possible? Some planters are not entirely color-blind, but are seemingly confused about the habits of plants when massed for color effect.

In one place a beautiful vase that formed a part of the general design of a pretty Moorish house, had been entirely covered with a clump of shrubs. Why an owner who had taste enough to demand a building of rare artistic design should permit one of its best features to be covered up with shrubbery, is hard to understand. Within a stone's throw, the owner of a pretty home had been fortunate (?) enough to have his entire lot surrounded by a border of shrubbery, which had been varied from a straight line by means of a few widenings, not unlike the swellings of a boa-constrictor after swallowing its prey. The general effect of such planting reminds one of a piece of ground from which the snow has been cleared off and piled up all around the edge. The old adage, "Plant thick and thin quick," is very good if strictly followed, but in the majority of places where no gardener is employed the thinning out is rarely done, and the outcome is a deplorable mass of crippled growth.

Perhaps sometime in the future the average lot owner will, through experience dearly bought, learn a lesson and appreciate good work. The new landscaper has very much in common with the well-known tree-butcher, and the sooner both disappear the better for the community.

URBAN AND SUBURBAN LANDSCAPE GARDENING

Park and Cemetery, March 1903

Landscape gardening is an art very little appreciated and less understood. This is largely due to the greater intelligence required to understand its ever-changing colors and forms and its breadth of view. It is a picture in the full sense of the term, but a living one and as such can not be composed of fixed colors and confined within a small frame like a painting.

There are many poor forms of either, but those of superior art are even admired by the uneducated; therefore, for the latter the art of landscape gardening shall exert its great influences. "Landscape gardening will develop until its powers to move the passions shall be equal to that of music." Landscape gardening as applied to the city or village is a subject of such great possibilities, that to give it a fair treatment would be impossible within the limits of this paper and I shall, therefore, restrict my remarks to the most important practical points. Architecture and the treatment of surrounding landscape must follow hand in hand whether we have to deal with it in the city or suburban town; but in the latter architecture must be subordinate to existing or prevailing landscape, whereas in the city landscape gardening is rather subordinate to architecture, the latter being the dominant factor.

Landscape gardening in the city is limited by a number of causes; first of all, space; second, soil and drainage, and third, polluted atmosphere. Each one of these will have to be consulted in the selection of planting material or failure is an assured fact. Let us first consider space. The ground available for planting is often limited to the narrow strip of land between the sidewalk and the street, known as the parkway. Its availability for planting is determined by its width and distance from adjoining buildings. There is very little chance, indeed, for any vegetation to grow where the building line has been established along the sidewalk edge, and this is greatly diminished on the south side of streets running east and west, and especially where eight or ten-story modern apartment buildings line the thoroughfare. Then add to this a street filled in with cinders and rubbish on the other side and you will admit that the chances for a tree to grow under such conditions are poor at the best, even if you have been generous enough to provide your nursling with a few loads of good soil.

Where a building or private house line has been established on the avenue there is usually room for planting inside the lot line besides on the parkway, and it is in such localities that some possibilities exist for landscape gardening.

Soil and drainage are great factors in tree growing. To plant a tree in ashes and tin cans with an asphalt pavement on one side and a cement sidewalk on the other and still expect it to grow is not an unusual thing. Nourishing food is the first principle of good health, whether it applies to vegetation or human life. Starvation means an easy victim to disease. As good soil is essential to success in tree culture so is drainage. This may exist naturally in gravelly or sandy soils, or artificially in the tiles or sewers. Where nature has provided proper drainage artificial drainage is not only superfluous but dangerous to tree growth. We have some good examples of this in the destruction of the once beautiful woodlands north and south of Chicago. Their disappearance is attributed to the sewers. But we must have sewers and we must have trees that will thrive in their vicinity. Is the sewer artificial so is the hose, and I say do not neglect to use it, especially where the street pavement consists of asphalt or brick, and every drop of rain is carried away into the sewer.

Irrigation by perforated tiles is the proper and only way to water street trees. That smoke and poisonous gases, characteristic of manufacturing towns, are dangerous to tree life you all know. Few, indeed, are the trees that will grow under these most trying conditions, but we are progressing fast and the city of the future will not have to fight the smoke nuisance.

All this tells us that in the city "countryfied"—which is our aim—we must select trees that will thrive under existing conditions. I doubt if we can find one that will grow on an ash heap. Where the surroundings are extremely unfavorable you may have to close your artistic eyes for the sake of getting some green leafage even if it is a promising weed. To select planting material for streets lined with tall buildings to the very edge of the sidewalk is quite difficult, as the space hardly permits the healthy development of any tree. The Lombardy poplar is too short lived, and the stately cypress will not grow here. The ash falls an easy victim to death-dealing insects and so does the silver maple. The linden and hard maple very seldom attain the desired height under such conditions; besides the first named demands particular soil for its healthy development. There is nothing left, so we will have to be satisfied with the elm as a cripple, or open our arms to the cottonwood. Whether a continuous planting of one variety of tree, or a change in the planting scheme every other or every second or third block is most desirable, is a matter of preference; but on main and continuous thoroughfares one variety is the most satisfactory. In the residence or better home district a varied planting scheme is more picturesque, but it should at all events be governed by the architecture most dominant. Old English and colonial imitation look well in a mixture of trees and shrubbery, and a liberal planting of climbing plants; while on the other hand, the gothic type and the pure colonial demands tall towering trees in contrast with its peaks and spires for the one and straight pillars for the other. Apropos of large trees—be judicious in their selection; their dominant qualifications are apt to prove injurious to other garden friends; besides how can we define the beauty of a tree when unable to look at it in the perspective? The large trees belong properly to the country, or large grounds, where they can receive the necessary nourishment for their full development and their majestic forms mingle so beautifully with the sky and surrounding landscape. The new post office in Chicago will serve as an illustration. What a pity that so much money should be wasted where a less expensive building would have done the same service. Just as well as a large tree needs room on which to show its beauty so does a building of monumental architecture. In most residence districts where the buildings have been placed the desirable distance from the street line and their character is one of subordination to the surroundings rather than one to attract attention on account of superior architecture, the rural aspect in the general planting scheme should prevail and is here the most pleasing. And what a variety of material to select from! It makes no difference whether your garden consists of clay or sand. There is enough for all. In the parkway and that part of the garden adjoining it we must have harmony and the simpler the planting the more beautiful it is. If there be a desire for variety and room for planting, keep it away from the street. Have your little arboretum at the rear of the house as a sort of museum, but do not let it get mixed up in the general planting scheme. One or several blocks can be planted for spring effect, another for fall colors, and so on. Imagine a street ablaze with pink and white in early May or a variety of red and yellow in October! Again referring to the gothic building style, straight avenues of elms or lindens are more fitting, and this class of architecture suggests a garden of a liberal mixture of foreign trees and shrubs. Before discussing suburban landscape gardening, let us understand that the suburban town is intermediate between city and country, and such should be the idea in its houses and gardens. Has the town site been selected on the treeless prairie, its development in landscape gardening will be largely due to the taste of the individual owners, if foresight has not committed the layout of the town to the hands of the landscape gardener before a single lot had been sold.

Was it the forest that attracted the city dweller as a desirable place for his home? Then his first love should dictate the character of building and landscape architecture. Although variety in the landscape is to some extent desired, it must first of all be in harmony with its surroundings, and the general planting scheme be one of a united whole, whether the town has developed among natural or artificial associations. The so-called park plans should prevail in the layout of a suburban town, but let us not despise a straight avenue now and then, and especially where the land is almost level and the vista perfect. On low lands the elm stands first as an avenue tree, and on high gravelly grounds none excels the hard or sugar maple. As has been previously mentioned, architecture must be governed by the natural surroundings, and that architect is wise who knows his limits. Perhaps in towns with entirely artificial surroundings his ingenious mind can be permitted greater sway, but he must at all times respect the rights of adjoining property and not disturb the general character that prevails. The color of buildings in relation to the landscape invariably tends to disturb or please the environments of a suburb. Brown or red colors in stone or brick mingle beautifully with the many varieties of reds and yellows in the fall landscape and are therefore best adapted among hardwood trees and their associations in shrubs and vines. On the other hand, light colors are more pleasing where green prevails, and especially among the evergreen forests. In the city, and more so in the villa, town garden walls or iron fences along the street border are an imposition upon true American ideals. Do not lock yourself up in an iron cage or imprison yourself behind towering walls; the days of barbarism and feudalism— their instigators—are past. Of course, some seclusion is needed, but there is plenty of live material that will lend itself to such a purpose and screen a low fence— if the latter is deemed necessary—and how beautiful, how restful and pleasing does it not look against the despotism-inspired wall or iron fence! Just imagine a street lined with walls and fences and one clothed in nature's beautiful covering, and compare the influence each is going to have on those that have to live amid such surroundings. How some people look upon these copied innovations is well shown in the following incident.

A few days ago my foreman passing a house entirely screened by a twelve-foot iron fence, naturally stopped to take in the sights, when he was approached by an elderly couple inquiring if he could tell them what institution it was and if it was an insane asylum. He, being a stranger himself, was not able to answer the query. If the character of the building is enhanced by a hedge, then by all means let us have one; harmony we must have at all hazards, but who will claim that a stone wall or iron fence adds to the beauty of the building? The invasion is here, but true Americanism will resist it—and will conquer in the end. Here on our great prairies, cradled by the balmy breezes of mid-summer, and the health, vigor and strength-giving northerner of mid-winter, broadened in conception by the great rolling plains, inspired by the pure atmosphere and clear, penetrating sky, American art will rise and spread its beneficent influence over the entire world.

Soil Conditions
and Tree Growth around
Lake Michigan, Part II

Park and Cemetery, May 1904

Few trees have such a wide distribution on the North American continent as the red cedar, and none shows a greater indifference to soil.

Although the red cedar is indifferent in its selection of soil, this does not mean that it is as prolific and produces such strong and healthy growth on rock formation or land ridges as on the more fertile lands.

In its northern course it gradually decreases in size and declines in vigor until the great tree of the south becomes a mere shrub.

In Northern Illinois and in Wisconsin the red cedar obtains its greatest size on eroded and terraced lake and river bluffs and is invariably most abundant on the sunny slopes. The soil is glacial drift (moraine) and consists of a yellow pebbly clay. It is not unusual to find trees a foot or more in diameter near the ground and from 20 to 25 feet high and in some instances more.

The American beech—Fagus ferruginea—is indigenous to Michigan and Wisconsin, and its distribution in both states is confined to lands originally glacial drift (moraine). In Illinois (same kind of soil) it is entirely absent or exists only in small groves. I know of but two, one at Highland Park and the other near the city of Waukegan.

The trees in both groups are small compared with those in Wisconsin, less than 25 miles farther north. Mr. Thomas Douglas of Waukegan believes that these groups were disseminated by pigeons who carried the seeds with them from the northern forests.

Whatever their origin one thing is certain that the beech in its natural or artificial distribution towards the head of Lake Michigan becomes smaller and less vigorous.

Trees planted in the same soil (moraine) more than 25 years ago within 15 miles of Chicago and near the lake, are still less than 15 feet in height with a diameter of not more than six inches near the ground. Any attempt to introduce this or any other variety of the beech on the plain (prairie) near Chicago has proved futile and only dwarf shrubby plants are the result where enough success has been obtained to make them live even for a short time.

Let us suppose that the beeches found in Illinois and referred to before were disseminated by the pigeons. Why did these birds that invaded localities farther south by the millions not drop seeds here too? Perhaps they did! Yet the absence of beeches here on soil favorable for their reproduction does not sustain this assertion. Soil and other conditions are not favorable to the beech on the prairie and if they had been the great prairie fires would have prevented their reproduction here, as it has done with other tree growth. As we proceed towards the north from the head of Lake Michigan the lands bordering the lake receive a greater benefit from the evaporation constantly going on from this great body of water and carried inland by the winds. This is especially true on the Michigan side.

But this dampness is also perceptible on the western side of the lake at considerable distances, and the influence of Lake Superior from the north becomes greater. Where conditions thus favored exist, we find the natural home of the American beech—within or near the borders of the celebrated white pine belt.

However, the influences of the dry prairie winds are more perceptible from the head of Lake Michigan west, and it can not be doubted that their influences upon vegetation is one of the primary causes of the exclusion of so many plants indigenous to the state east of us, and in their western course have penetrated the very limits of the city of Chicago.

Hawthorns in the Landscape

Park and Cemetery, May 1904

Bordering the open prairie or skirting the meadows one invariably finds the hawthorns (Crataegus) singly or in groups.

They, together with the crab apple (Pyrus coronaria) and wild Plum (Prunus americana), are the making of such a landscape; this quiet, peaceful and simple, yet wonderfully inspiring scene is characteristic of the plains of the temperate zones.

Their low spreading heads, their almost horizontal branches, melt into the broad, level stretches and teach us a lesson in the composition of landscape.

Harmonious and beautiful in outlines; exhilarating and inspiring during the flowering period, and picturesque and captivating when covered with myriads of vividly-colored fruits, nature has performed this work in a masterly manner.

Beauty and simplicity are inseparable. No June bride was ever more beautifully adorned than the meadows wreathed with the white blossoms of the hawthorn.

We may roam in Italian gardens and French promenades, but Nature helps the gardener that values and feels the masterly art portrayed in this landscape. The May-day meadow, brightened by countless phloxes and framed so modestly by hawthorn, crab apple, wild plum, black haw and dogwood, or in autumn, when field and forest are afire, how well the scarlet berries of the hawthorn fit into the glorious mixture of golden rod, maple and oak. Later in the season, when snow and ice have covered brook and meadow, the gray-colored bark of the hawthorn gently softens the dark, gloomy forest edge, forming a happy union of wood and meadow.

But with all the soft and mellow lines due its character, there is strength, tenacity and durability in its general make-up. No wonder that the hawthorn is found among the forerunners and pioneers of the forest. He is one of those children of our landscape that give it national character; yet—how deplorable—like the aborigines, almost despised....

LANDSCAPE ART—
AN INSPIRATION FROM THE
WESTERN PLAINS

The Sketch Book: A Magazine Devoted to the Fine Arts, September 1906

Broadly speaking this is the beginning of the American Renaissance, the constructive period in more than one art. From a western view it is pioneer life. The composer tries to form his composition from real life as he sees it on our plains. His material is more than interesting, but as his art is in the developing stage, false notes appear constantly to his mind; his compositions are subject to them. He, himself, is a part of the existing conglomeration. Pitched to the highest key, such real life of the West may at times fall into a chaos of uncertainty not unlike the blending together of a dozen races in chorus. His markings may be few but they count nevertheless, and are destined to become part of a great and beautiful composition, national in product but international in character.

Landscape art is subject to such influences as religion and climatic conditions. These direct the habits and customs of the people. Harmony in composition is as essential in landscape art as in music. It must talk to us and inspire the soul with good. It must be lovely, fascinating and sublime, yet quiet, restful and dignified in its make-up, awakening the finer senses to the noblest of impulses.

Landscape is seen at its best in the home and its surroundings. More thought has, perhaps, been bestowed upon the garden. Our gardens should reflect our lives; they should be a part of us, a part of our material and spiritual life. They should be a part of the landscape expressing those things which we admire and worship. Unpretentious, free from arrogant and vulgar expression, simple, charming, lovely, full of poetry and music, the composition must be perfect.

Harmony in colors is essential. There is delight and joy in a perfect color contrast against a green background. There is purity in the quiet pool of crystal water and in the snow white lilies. There is music in the dropping water supplying the pool. There is poetry in the virgin bower safely hanging over the rocky ledge where tall lilies vie with the waters of the hurrying brook beneath for a place behind dark, secluded cedars. There is inspiration in it all! And above all, the garden walk, which has been remembered in song and story and picture from time immemorial. A happy medium of distinct character and fascination, expressing well the old adage that there is nothing in this world worth having that does not cost some trouble.

To preserve and refine that which nature has so generously given us and to which we should show our reverence, that which no human hand can duplicate and only the higher intelligence appreciate, that is our duty.

The meadow landscape must be beautiful in spring like the song of the bird, quiet during the hot summer days and full of splendor when bidding us goodbye for winter rest. The parting tone, the grand encore, assisted, as it were, by the afterglow of the setting sun, produces one of the grandest panoramas of our prairie landscape.

The meadow is the bright spot of the North, reflecting light and sunshine. It has forever become an indispensable part of the home of the North—the only place in the world where real home sentiment exists. The home is sacred to those so fortunate as to have it; it is their own, the most precious and beautiful possession any mortal being can claim. This sentiment must be reflected by the artist, the desire of seclusion and privacy, but without destroying the beauty from without.

The material at the disposal of the artist is wonderful— land, sea, sky, with everchanging colors and varied sky lines, reflecting light and shade in endless variety. A beautiful picture must excel in good forms and color. Nothing is so fascinating as the light behind immediate shade; the lining to the cloud; to some, the hope beyond, which may be the greatest part of life itself; with its allurement of mystery, its enticement for reaching the goal beyond, yet withal, the futility of the effort, the inborn, onward striving of the soul toward the unattainable.

Every nation develops its own art. We are young as a nation and still in the process of crystallization. Every race or nationality brings to us some of its customs and habits which are gradually but surely being molded together, ultimately to form one national character. The environs amongst which the immigrants settle lend their great influence—sung by the poet, painted by the painter and idealized by the gardener.

The West is full of great possibilities, great, strong, fertile, with the right zest and thrill in its make-up. The atmosphere is pure and penetrating. There is no sleeping zephyr, but wide-awake blizzards and health-bringing summer breezes. Life, health and energy everywhere abound. What a glorious country from which to draw inspiration! This great prairie landscape, with the wonderful Rocky Mountains as its setting to the West and the Father of Rivers flowing through its fertile valleys. Its destiny is great— yes! and from this grand landscape we draw our inspiration.

SOME GARDENS OF
THE MIDDLE WEST

The Architectural Review, May 1908

Gardens are jewels set in the great out-of-doors, studded over the surface of the earth according to the refinement and wealth of the different races and nations; for refinement and wealth are both necessary to create beautiful surroundings. Wealth gives time and leisure to acquire culture and refinement, and with the advancement of both refinement and wealth on our great plains, the first gardens appear. Unassuming, simple in design, democratic as our people, full of inspiration drawn from the great plains, they spring up—scattered over the broad expanse of prairie, wherever refinement and wealth are manifest.

The forest, stately and sublime, with its beautiful floral matting; the meadows, painted over by Nature's delicate hand; the rippling brook, overflowing with life,— all lend their charm and influence to the building of our gardens. Gardens of flowers first, in harmony—a happy and ideal brotherhood of friends; then architecture, subservient to them; and water—the symbol of purity, cooling and refreshing in midsummer, with its misty spray, enchanting against the dark green of the mystic cedar; or, as a mirror, with the reflection of horizontal cloud effects on a quiet summer's day—like the lines of the plains themselves; or reflecting the passing shadows of hurrying, rolling *cumuli* as the great western wind whirls new life and energy into the drowsy mind, depicting so well the rolling plains that we love;—all these, reflected in the pool—an ideal pot of color and landscape

The garden is a shrine amongst its surroundings—not a gaudy show-place that must constantly change color and form like the ever-changing attractions of Coney Island. For the purpose of the garden is to be charming, restful, soul-inspiring—not "attractive," as this has no connection with art.

As, at the opening of a Wagnerian opera, the high note of the introduction thrills through our nerves, so must the dominant note of the garden appear from its very gateway.

Garden gates entering from the home are forbidding. There is freedom in the open gateway, which, marked with stately urns, lends refinement to the garden.

Flowing water likewise has its charm at the garden entrance, anticipating so well the purity of what one expects to find beyond.

Full of poetry as the garden itself is the garden wall. It lends the secrecy of home, and offers protection from biting late spring winds, or the winter's unmerciful cold. With delicious fruit trained on it, it answers a useful purpose; while it delights the eye and soul with rambling vines and stately hollyhocks to soften the rigid lines of brick and mortar, or, better still, a wall of lilacs, double flowering almond, Chinese cherries, or sweetbriar and prairie roses—a living hedge surrounding the garden, whose full beauty we may admire and enjoy as a thing apart.

Arbors, garden houses, and garden seats make the garden habitable, and invite us to linger in the pure and fragrant atmosphere. The garden seat serves two purposes, with arbor combination,—a cooling retreat on a hot day; and at night, illumined by the softened rays of the garden lamp, what more ideal place for study or reading could be desired!

The vine-covered arbor, particularly inviting in the silvery moonlight, and the garden house, where friends may meet in pleasant intercourse,—have both a tendency to uplift and transport man's thought into a higher sphere.

The garden walk takes us to the arbor, the garden house, and the garden seat. A clean path, of weather-worn brick, bordered with flowers or hedges, natural or trimmed, leading to the rest-inviting arbor, or winding away in the distance to "who knows where,"—interspersed with vases, urns, or statuary,—just as life itself, becomes the link between house and garden, a gradual and harmonious step from architecture to nature. Its long perspective is in common with the far-off view on the level plains, customary to the plainsman's eye.

Thus we build our gardens for the refined-wealthy; and thus we also build gardens for the refined-poor—whether they may be able to fully appreciate them at once or not. Let us call the latter "community gardens;" for they are gardens for the entire community,—for those who have no other gardens except their window-sills. There is no difference between these types, private and public, except that the latter should be more habitable. Both have the same purpose,—to uplift, to inspire. Upon the "community garden" falls the greatest burdens. It gives something to the people—indispensable to the full enjoyment of life—which they would otherwise have to be without.

These gardens have received favorable and unfavorable comment. The question arises whether it is perhaps wrong, or at least futile, to give colors to the public for their souls to feast upon, when there exists just cause of doubt as to their appreciation. Here is the answer:

I was recently glancing through the window of a pioneer limited to the passing landscape for inspiration; but my eye instead encountered nothing but gray, gray clouds and gray fields, with corn everywhere; for miles and miles nothing but prairie, nothing but corn, not even an interesting hamlet or a glimpse of color, yet I was not conscious of the need until I entered my host's garden. Then what a relief!

Is it not reasonable to expect a thirst for color among the dwellers in piles of stone and mortar, begrimed with soot and dust? The measure of color should be dealt out with intelligence, with no "attractions," only color and harmony; nothing to irritate, but everything to soothe and inspire; gardens of color, strong enough in character and design to impress one at once with their beauty and refinement; to command our respect and admiration, as it were, so that the soul may be imbued with the desire to protect and appreciate these nature spots rather than to mutilate or trample them.

Harmony in color is essential, and the effect of contrasting colors is felt and appreciated, whether understood or not.

We may well compare gardens and their composition with music: one garden may be likened to Sousa, another to Wagner, each expressing its particular motif. Thus the educational force is felt, and that is what our community gardens must be— educational.

But our ideal gardens are yet to come. The task is too great for one mind. All forces of American art must unite harmoniously, and then the garden of the Middle West will rise in a new and more beautiful form. We are but dreaming of what the future will bring to us,—listening to the invigorating winds that sweep down from the lofty peaks of the western mountains, brushing across the Great Valley of the Father of Waters; listening with keen interest to what they have to say from hills and valleys, lakes and plains. But we also rise on tiptoe to look over the Alleghenies, and the Rocky Mountains, for inspiration from the very cradles of civilization.

IMPROVING A SMALL COUNTRY PLACE

Illinois Outdoor Improvement Association, January 1910

As an enforced city-dweller, it seems to me few rarer pleasures can come to a man of moderate means than the getting and the development of a country place—no matter how modest its proportions may be. The more unformed the materials he finds in his hands, the greater his opportunity to express his own individuality and personal taste in the work.

But, whether his tastes are formed or unformed, he is liable to fall into mistakes which will remain as scars to mar his creation for years to come unless he works in harmony with certain basic principles of landscape gardening—principles all too little understood, even by those who assume professional familiarity with them. It is my purpose in this paper briefly to suggest these principles or to illustrate them by simple working rules.

In speaking of a small country place I have in mind an area of about three acres—certainly not less than one acre and from that up to five.

Naturally, the first thing to consider is the topography, the "lay of the land," and the next is the actual building site. Fortunate is the man who finds himself in possession of a site having a natural elevation and one which will permit him a south or an east frontage—or both—with space for a generous lawn or meadow before the house. Often the man whose means are limited has to content himself with something far less ideal than this—with, perhaps, an old house already "rooted" to an ill-chosen site looking to the west or north. If so, he must make the best of a bad bargain—which need not be so very bad, after all!

If, however, he is privileged to build his own house he should plan it in harmony with the character of country in which he lives; and, as probably most readers of this paper dwell in a comparatively flat or gently rolling country, it may be assumed that the prairie landscape is the most representative. A house of long and simple lines is the only one which really harmonizes with the wide skies and the far-stretching and severe landscape of the prairies.

Let us start with the supposition that the main rooms of the house look out upon the east and south; that in these directions there is space reserved for an eye-filling lawn or meadow sloping to the street. The driveway by which entrance is to be had to the place is, perhaps, the next feature to consider. Unless the grounds are really ample, it will be necessary to plan the driveway so that it will take up as little space as possible, and, at the same time, give a graceful and pleasing effect. Therefore, it should approach the house on a curve, for the drive which goes straight *at* a house gives the most rigid, unvaried and altogether uninviting prospect possible. A simple semicircle, therefore, is the best arrangement, or a circular turn in front of the door—a splendid place for a pool or a fountain if water is plentiful. Sometimes a variation will be necessary. At any rate, the driveway should approach the house indirectly, and should swing alongside the entrance door instead of having the effect of running into it.

The charm and convenience of a house of long and simple lines, and, therefore, thoroughly in harmony with the best modern architecture, will be greatly enhanced by an open terrace, and, if practicable, a water-basin of simple design. Well-chosen urns, filled with flowering plants, fit in most harmoniously with this architectural and landscape scheme; they may be used in the place of the water-basin or as accessories to it.

In some instances a terrace may do away with the necessity, and even the desirability, for anything in the nature of a formal flower-garden in the front prospect. If a terrace is not possible, something of the same pleasing effect may be secured by appropriate porches. In fact, the spacious porch has the right to come into rank as a cardinal necessity of the country house. Any observer of country life cannot fail to see that no part of the house is more used in summer than the cool, clean, inviting porch, covered with vigorous climbers.

The Vegetable Garden the Prime Delight

Convenience dictates that the vegetable garden—and no country house should be thought of without this prime delight of country living—should be placed in the rear of the grounds so as to be easily accessible from the kitchen. But it should also be accessible from the terrace. Many considerations of utility suggest this, besides the fact that one of the first places to which your guests will direct their footsteps is the garden. It is the retreat to which all comers inevitably gravitate.

A brick walk with an arbor effect makes the most fascinating link possible between the terrace or lawn at the front and the garden in the rear. A walk leading to a garden should never be made of any material save brick. It satisfies the artistic sense and invites the footsteps with promises of pleasant vistas beyond the possibilities of any other material. Besides, it is thoroughly serviceable. Concrete is harsh, forbidding and commercial by comparison with brick for this particular use.

As to the arbor itself, let the planting be of grapes, for they serve both the purposes of beauty and utility, and in the season of bloom they till the air with a fragrance more rare and delicious than that of almost any purely ornamental flower. Of course, there are many places where the climate is too harsh and the location too exposed for the successful growing of grapes, but with a little care the vines may be made to thrive and give a rich arbor-covering where the fruitage is meager. As to the matter of soil, that may easily be made in sufficient quantity to serve, without regard to the character of your land as a whole. But, if your conditions seem too hostile for grapes as an arbor-covering, there are various agreeable substitutes. Among these I would suggest our native fox-grape, Japanese or common bittersweet—charming in summer and winter.

Along those portions of this walk not covered by the arbor should be planted a border of herbaceous perennials, and here and there should be set an ornamental urn, with its overflowing burden of bloom and fragrance. Of course, a few pieces of statuary give to the landscape of a country home a dignity and refinement not obtainable by any other means; but worthy statuary is expensive and few owners of small country places can afford it. The garden walk may lead to a seat covered by trailing roses— a delightful spot for an hour's repose in the garden.

Next comes the question of a garden wall. If your purse can possibly compass it, by all means have a wall to the north and west, for it brings to you the most charming possibilities. The growing of choice wall fruit is one of the rarest delights of a small country place. Besides, the garden wall will shelter your regular vegetable, small-fruit and flower garden from the cold north and northwest winds, giving you a far earlier, choicer and more abundant fruitage—and with less labor and care.

The cost of a wall of this kind may be reduced to a very reasonable sum. If the owner of the place is of a mechanical turn and wishes to find exercise and recreation in manual labor he may, with a little practice, learn how to build a simple wall with his own hands. Or, possibly, he may have access to a day laborer who is equal to this task. Again, he may greatly reduce the cost of his wall by picking up a bargain in old brick, either from a demolished building in his town, from a contractor or from a regular wrecking company. Of course, if he were going to lay anything but a rough wall he would find that the extra labor required to trim the mortar from the old bricks would bring the cost up to nearly or quite that of new brick; but the garden wall may be laid very roughly, and be quite as artistic and sufficiently strong.

USES AND BEAUTIES OF GARDEN WALLS

There is more charm, it seems to me, in growing the rarest flowers. A luscious peach, pear, apricot, or apple which has reached its perfection of flavor, color and size because it has been grown against the sheltering and supporting breast of a garden wall—shielded from chilling winds and nurtured with unstinted floods of sunlight until it blushes with color and exudes fragrance—is a more beautiful thing in my eyes, than the rarest orchid; and I believe that any country dweller who will plant and train a fruit tree against his own garden wall and watch the development of the luscious globes of fruit will certainly share this feeling. . . .

Peaches are undoubtedly the easiest to grow in this way—and, perhaps, the most beautiful and satisfactory. Cherries, pears, apples and plums rank next, with apricots in the difficult list. To prevent the burning of trees when the summer sun is fiercest, any variety of close-clinging creepers may be first planted against the wall and the fruit trees trained over this cool and protecting cushion of vines. Screens of cheap white cotton cloth stretched on light frames may also be used. . . . They have the advantage of being inexpensive and easily removable. The charm of a garden wall trained with peaches, plums, apples and other fruits is only to be realized by an actual view of it; the best photograph can only tamely suggest its beauties because the glow of color is lacking. From the earliest springtime appearing of bud and leaf to the falling of verdure in autumn, these trees of the garden wall are of unfailing delight to the eye. . . .

To permit an easy and convenient cultivation, the arrangement of a vegetable garden must be rigid and formal; ovals, curves and "natural" groupings of beds are forbidden by the difficulties which add to the labor of the gardener; therefore, the problem is to give as much grace, beauty and softness as possible to lines necessarily severe and harsh.

This is best done by a neat arrangement of paths bordered with the various kinds of berry bushes and by flowers from which to cut blooms for table and house decoration. Blackberries, raspberries and other fruit bushes needing a little support may be so trained as to form an attractive hedge with which to screen the vegetable beds or frame the garden. But, if something more ornamental is desired, a low privet hedge, of the hardy Japanese varieties, is still more beautiful and frames the garden in a most charming way. However, the border of small fruit bushes has the advantage of affording special facility for picking the fruit from the paths. And the same convenience is served in the borders of flowers.

Returning to the details of the grounds in front, let me remark that it is important that the lawn or meadow be fairly level—or rather smooth—without hillocks or holes, and its slopes and surfaces in keeping with the topography of the general locality. . . .

FRAMING THE LAWN IN HARMONIOUS GREENERY

Above all, this lawn or stretch of grass should be framed in vegetation indigenous to the country, and in harmony with the architecture of the house and other buildings, and with the general character of the surrounding landscape. In other words, all the parts of your landscape creation should be harmonious as a whole and so placed as to conform to the environment in which they are created. For example, I have often seen bottom-land vegetation used in the ornamentation of an elevation or a hillside, and trees and shrubs which Nature plants only on high land placed by so-called landscape gardeners in low, wet places and along the border of streams. This is unfit and incongruous, running counter to the plain laws of natural selection, aside from all chances of success.

Perhaps more mistakes are made along this line than any other in the treatment of small country places.

A kindred and almost equally common error is the importation of shrubs and trees, the use of stock which is not indigenous or has not proved adapted to those parts where it is to be planted. When we look out upon our garden friends, we wish to see them thriving and contented, at home in a congenial atmosphere and environment—strong, hearty and beautiful. . . . What do those who have imported their garden friends look out upon?—those who have brought the bright things of another zone into forced and uncongenial exile! Generally, they see their landscape marred by the presence of dwarfs, cripples and delinquents from the flora of another clime. And, at best, they are as sadly out of place as would be a gazelle from Africa among the animals of a New England farm!

This is just as absurd as it would be to build a house in pure Italian Renaissance style and then fill it with curios from Japan, China and the islands of the South Seas. Perhaps the easiest way in which to get the true perspective on this important matter is to consider how your place would look in the eyes of a guest from some foreign land—a visitor of refined and artistic tastes who had come to look at your garden as something representative of America and of your own particular part of your country. Would he find anything to admire in it if it were crowded with waifs and strays from various countries—and sickly ones at that? Nothing! His artistic sense would be offended, and he would also have the right to assume that you were decidedly lacking in true American spirit.

VEGETATION THAT IS DELICATE AND CHARMING

Then let us remember that the man who plants his garden with imported stock is almost certain to see it in ruin before he leaves it. And we have no need to look elsewhere for the richest and the loveliest planting material. Not only is our vegetation delicate and charming in springtime, but it is also most beautiful in fall. Our autumnal foliage is not surpassed in the glory and the variety of its colors by that of any country in the world. And at no season (save at midwinter) is it less attractive than may be found in any foreign land.

All this to emphasize the keynote of this message on the development of a small country place: In choosing your materials keep ever in mind the purpose to make it thoroughly consistent and typical of your own country and your own locality.

Coming now to the definite details of planting, remember that it is well to make all your lines as undulating as possible. This puts more notes into your picture, more light and shade, makes it more varied and restful. You will need to give special thought to your sky-lines—if you are fortunate enough to have control of them. Let them be soft and undulating. And plant to the same purpose when the background of your foliage is to be the greensward, the site of a building or the waters of a river or lake. You will be astonished, in time, at the charm which the following of this simple rule will bring to your outlook.

As the spring delights us most after the long rest of winter, you should not neglect to give special consideration, in choosing shrubs and trees, to select a goodly complement of those which are calculated to delight the heart of spring. Be generous with the beautiful wild crabs, hawthorns, plums and other lovely wild things which made the prairies of springtime sweet and inviting to the pioneers who settled the Western country. What petaled creation of the Japanese garden is more appealing to the eyes than close, low wild crab, with its charming pink bloom, or the red haw with its flat roof of foliage to which summer will bring bands of foraging boys to feast upon its miniature scarlet apples, pink of flesh and flavored with the very aroma of the prairies? The spiraea is another springtime favorite which should not be neglected for those who delight in the spring landscape.

Then, for later pleasure, provide borders of native roses backed by tall shrubs. Of these the June berry, the sheepberry, the sumac and the black haw are my favorites. You will find them in plenty, I doubt not, along your own country roads and in the woods of neighboring farms, so their only cost will be that of transplanting. And, if you hunt them yourself and have a personal part in their moving, you will have far greater pleasure in their growth than if these labors are delegated to another. I cannot pass the question of indigenous shrubs without special mention of the sumac—the most superbly decorative as well as, perhaps, the most abundant of all the beautiful low-growing things with which Nature has strewn our highways and clearings. Money cannot buy from the importing nurseryman any lovelier shrub than our sumac.

Trees should be planted in scattering groups—not too thickly, for overcrowding is a common and disastrous fault. Red oaks, hard maples, red maples, birches, native cherries, beech, tulip, sassafras, sycamore, linden, buckeye, pepperidge, walnut, butternut, ash and the native elms are the best trees for liberal use, in accordance with their adaptation to the situation selected for them. In association with the house, the homelike, sheltering make-up of the elm is not surpassed by any other tree. A plantation of these varieties is not only a harmony of color in itself, but it is also fitting for our landscape—delicately beautiful in spring; quiet, restful and cooling in the hot days of summer; and as charming in autumn as a winter sunset on the Western plains.

A liberal planting of shrubbery will serve as a protection to the trees, and shrubbery does not suffer so much by the process of thinning and removal as do trees. Where evergreens thrive it is well to introduce them sparingly at the entrance gates—the best material for a natural gateway—as screens for the barn, garage or other outbuildings, and in border plantations where their striking contrast of growth and foliage will not mar the general harmony. For light-and-shade effects there is nothing in the evergreen family to compare with the green form of the blue spruce and the beautiful red cedar.

Whether by reason of its color or its peculiar growth, there is something inde-scribably mystical and weird about the red cedar, and among evergreens there is no possible grouping more charming than produced by the right use of this enchanting tree; and what warmth and charm they give to our winter landscape!

In an occasional nook or corner plant a few low-creeping junipers, mixed with herbaceous perennials and lilies, and the effect will captivate the eye of the most critical. The combination is little short of irresistible.

Vines take the harshness from the walls and are easily grown, and a few shrubs to round off the sharp corners bring house and garden together in a harmonious whole. Perhaps the most serviceable of these is Engelmann's creeper and . . . Boston creeper. A lovely effect is secured by intertwining either of these with a hardy clematis.

Ruddy Berries to Bespeak Hospitality

Winter is the last season to be considered in planting—and the last to be neglected! Along the brick walk connecting the house with the street make your border plantation of barberries, high-bush cranberries, Indian currants and snowberries. Your selection of these for the entrance and borders should be made with proper regard for the harmony of their summer dress with the foliage of adjacent shrubs and trees. When the landscape is clothed in the severity of its winter draperies, the bright and ruddy berries of these shrubs are present to give cheery greeting to all who enter driveway or walk. . . .

It is not wholly extravagant to speak of the fireplace as the sanctuary of the house—of the interior of the country home in season of chill and cold. The same term may with equal fitness be applied to the pool of water in the grounds of the country home in the season of heat. The very sight of it is refreshing and delightful. . . . So, if Nature has not given your country place a prospect which affords at least a glimpse of water, supply the deficiency with an artificial pool, if your purse will possibly permit. It will yield delight and refreshment and be a jewel in your little landscape creation.

Consideration should also be given the service yard, either framed in with tall-growing lilacs, evergreens or, if space is wanting, a trellis covered with rapid-growing creeper, or a plaster or brick wall. If a service road is desirable have it well hidden with a mixed plantation of trees and shrubs.

Should the lot be part of the forest, the introduction of a campfire surrounded by rustic seats or box seats filled with pine needles and entered by a winding trail will be an interesting feature. . . . This campfire will add many pleasant hours of all sorts of entertainments to those that delight in this historic relic of pioneer life. Colonies of wild flowers should be planted along the trail and scattered through the grove.

The main principles of art are simplicity and good composition, and, in giving these suggestions to those who are happily burdened with the development of a small country place, I have sought to bear in mind this fact, and it should never for a moment be lost sight of by any who may seek to make practical application of those principles and rules which I have tried to make clear.

REGULATING CITY BUILDING

The Survey, November 1911

Americans are continually criticized for their lack of conservatism, for their temporary enthusiasms which sweep the country like the prairie winds and leave no permanent effect. When we regard professional efforts as they are being directed along so-called new lines of activity, this criticism seems to be not without justification. Just now, city planning is rapidly rising on the wave of popular enthusiasm. It has taken our cities by storm. A new profession has come into life. Plans are rapidly being made, and the zealous public, gazing upon their depiction of gayly colored parks, wide boulevards, and ornate bridges, is fired with the desire to make all American cities such pleasing pictures as the clever draughtsman has represented on paper. But it is too much to assume that our cities can be transformed as quickly as the paper receives the ink of the enthusiastic designer, nor is it to be expected that the lines so cleverly laid down by the rule can be as readily cut through the physical complexities of a great city. Our laws do not give arbitrary power as do those of some European cities, and on account of this the immediate effects of our planning must fail. To cut a broad street through the city is one thing, to have the sides of it lined with buildings of a harmonious façade is another, and on this last depends a satisfactory working out of the plan; but where is the law to provide for this?

On the face of it, this idea of city planning is a fine thing—broad boulevards, ornate arches, formal promenades, all give one a feeling of excitement, as of being dressed in one's best clothes for some festive occasion. But right here is one of the most salient evils of such a city. It is too often a show city; it is at once the city of palaces and of box-like houses where humanity is packed together like cattle in railroad cars. To build civic centers and magnificent boulevards, leaving the greatest part of the city in filth and squalor, is to tell an untruth, to put on a false front, which vitiates the whole atmosphere of the town. The formal show environment reacts upon the people: the spirit of being on parade, of striving always for superficialities, makes of them a city of spendthrifts desirous of a gay life. As a consequence, immorality, strife, and discontent grow. The formal show city is distinctly imperialistic. It is undemocratic and its tendencies are destructive to the morals of its people. The more formality in design the less democracy in its feeling and tendency.

A show city is supposed to have a commercial value and, indeed, such a city will attract crowds to view its splendors and spend their money; but like the show itself, it needs constant variation or it becomes tiresome and loses its drawing qualities—it must have a new dress every so often, in order to entertain its crowds of visitors. But is the American city to be a commercial proposition with no other interest in its own people? Or is it to be a city of ideal homes, with a healthful expression of its business life? The American home is the foundation upon which the world's greatest democracy rests. It is the unit, of which the city is made up, and in it should center the whole force of city planning, in order to foster the highest ideals in its people, and to be an expression of the best in mankind. A city should first of all, then, be home-like. May not this be secured by a system of regulation?

Such regulation of the city might be in the hands of a new department, a department of civics, consisting of the best talent in art and science which the community possesses. Such a department might be made up of an engineer, an architect, a good business man, a sculptor, a landscape architect—the number depending upon the particular conditions of the individual city, and the vocations of the members to be a far less important consideration in determining membership than their public spirit. The members should be appointed a period of not less than six years, one member retiring every year, and their removal from office should be subject to judicial inquiry. This department would guide, advise, adjust, and pass upon all matters pertaining to the building of our cities and their extension through the purchase of land, new subdivisions, or the annexation of suburbs. Every expression of city development would be directed along the best possible lines by men fitted to consider not only artistic but utilitarian stand-points as well. It would pass upon transportation facilities, depot and freight yard terminals, harbor and river development, markets, lighting, and bridges. Designs for all municipal buildings, building sites, and public works of art would be submitted to it for approval. It would give advice in regard to the location and design of churches, clubs, hospitals, and depots, encouraging centers where an association of buildings is possible. Through conference with the civic board of control, each new public building erected would be constructed with a view to improving the city as a whole. No additional funds would be necessary to effect this; the buildings would cost no more than under the old scheme, but they would be located and planned with the help of the best authorities, not only with the special requirements of the buildings but with the good of the entire city under consideration. The services of the department of civics would be at the disposal of the public and semi-public corporations, and it would offer to promoters suggestions concerning prospective factories both as to situation and design, thus improving not only the sanitary conditions of the factory and its environs, but making it an interesting note in the city as well. It would prevent tenement housing through law or honest taxation, and promote cleanliness and health through our urban life. The department of civics would determine the width of streets and sidewalks with the future development of the city in view. A practical suggestion on this question of street widening might not be amiss at this point. It can be accomplished gradually by establishing a new curb line as a street changes from a residence to a business district, thus avoiding the great cost involved in condemning and moving expensive business buildings. Guided by the most competent of its citizens the city would improve step by step, day by day, in a sane and natural manner, rather than in the spasmodic spurts which result from business booms.

One of the most important duties of the board of civic control would be to develop the school as a neighborhood center, to unite home life with that of the school, to make the school a place of interest for both young and old. It is here that the boy and girl receive some of their most lasting impressions; the school is the point about which their early associations cluster; there is no reason why it should not continue to be a center of culture and healthful recreation throughout their lives, and remain as a pleasant spot to which they may return when old. Here recreation which left to itself is liable to take vicious forms could be made an uplifting influence. By providing halls for music, lectures, dancing and the production of plays, higher tastes could be cultivated. If the same authority which provides schools for the children is giving the father and mother an enjoyable evening full of color and music, it follows that the parents will be more interested in what their children are doing. Their whole field of interests is going to be bettered and at the same time united with that of their children.

The playground also would be established as a part of this neighborhood center. It belongs to the school and should not be conducted as a separate institution. Each gains from an association with the other. The playground gives the school building a setting which it too often lacks, and forms a kind of outdoor gymnasium....

Public and semi-public buildings such as churches, settlements, and club halls should form a part of the neighborhood center. They would here secure breadth and beauty of surroundings, add their quota of interest to the center, and serve the people to far greater advantage than when situated in a less accessible spot. These centers of enlightenment must be developed if our cities are to produce a people who will become a real factor in the progress of the world.

Another relation which should be established in the improved city is a union of home and workshop. Separation of factory and home means a greater breach between capital and labor, an opportunity for militant defense in time of strike which causes defiant spirit. It means as well greater congestion in our streets and reduced vitality for the workman. Travel for long distances on crowded cars tires him out, and makes him indifferent to healthful pleasure during his free hours. He has not enough strength left for the much needed outing with the family. Wholesome pleasure of this sort is essential to a right development of mind and body in the making of fit citizens for the republic. The union of factory and home means first of all better relations between employer and employee, it means more sanitary factory surroundings and more healthful interiors, together with greater effort for good design in the buildings. The factory as a building should become an important consideration in the city landscape, instead of giving rise to the smoky, unsightly communities that exist in so many instances. If properly located and designed there is no reason why it should not become a picturesque part of the city. Here again a center may be formed. Several factories may locate together about a square with its public fountain and parkway. The square affords a setting for the factory buildings and gives so much more light and healthful air to the employees. With the improved factory surroundings the task of uniting home and factory becomes comparatively simple. The factor which is able to effect this union is electricity; through it we may return to the same conditions, though on a larger and more improved scale, which existed between workmen and shop before machinery was invented. Next to the school center in importance to the modern city, artistically and socially, stands the factory center. Other centers to be developed are the depot center, the market center, etc.

To further every movement that stands for a better city—to make our cities more livable, home-like, places for all our people, especially for those who through the force of circumstances must endure the city year around—proper regulation guided by high ideals and common sense ought to be effective.

The melting pot is still boiling, American character still in making. We may plan cities for the future; but how many of these plans will be accepted by the Americans to come is a question. We cannot say to future generations, "Build thus and so"; but by careful regulation we can build our present-day cities in the spirit of sound and wholesome democracy which is the best foundation for the future.

TESTIMONY REGARDING PROPOSED SAND DUNES NATIONAL PARK

Report on the Proposed Sand Dunes National Park, Indiana, 1917

Mr. Secretary, ladies, and gentlemen . . . there should be no question at all about this dune park proposition. Just think of us poor prairie folks, who have not the Adirondack Mountains. . . . The only thing in the world that we have that has any similarity at all to the Adirondacks and the Rocky Mountains is our dunes over in Indiana. The 200 feet of Mount Tom look just as big to me as the Rocky Mountains did when I visited them some years ago, and bigger to me in fact, than did the Berkshires when I made my pilgrimage to those wonderful hills of Massachusetts. [Applause.] We need the dunes. If you had been with me yesterday and stood on top of one of the great blowouts, as we term them, and looked into the golds, the reds, the soft tinges of brown, and the soft shades of green that were just visible in some of those dune woods, you would have come back to your home saying, "We need the dunes; we can never do without them. We who live in the midst of this conglomeration of buildings, cement sidewalks, and stone pavements, how can we ever be without such a wonderful vision, a vision that we carry vividly with us until we can make our next pilgrimage?" If you had gone with me along one of the ancient trails, between Michigan City and Chicago, among those giant pines—I call them giant pines, because they are that way to me, and to all of us poor prairie folk in Illinois—you would have come back to your home saying, "Never, never must those wonderful pines be destroyed." The whole city of Chicago, and those people who live in our adjoining towns, as well as our good friends in Indiana, should become acquainted with that country in order that they may refresh themselves and revivify their souls.

It was many years ago that I made my first pilgrimage to the dunes. It was previous to the time our good friend Mather accompanied me. I can never describe to you the impression I received on the occasion of my first visit; but I will tell you this, the impression received yesterday, even after having gone through the dunes for more than 20 long years, was the greatest and most wonderful impression that I ever received there. I would give anything if I could only impart that wonderful impression, that wonderful feeling, to any one of you. It is something that will stay with me as long as I live. Those are the things for which the dunes stand and which make them of such value to us. There are lots of folk who say, "Well so many of us do not see these wonderful things." Oh, how materialistic we are. There is a soul in each of us and it only needs awakening; and when it is awakened then there will burst upon us the first realization of the wonderful beauty of the dune country. Suppose there are only a few of us who can see those wonderful things. That is to be regretted. But suppose the great painter, the master painter, sees them. Suppose the master poet sees them. I had the profound pleasure of spending an evening recently with Rabindranath Tagore, the Indian poet, who has seen wonderful and beautiful things such as these in far-off India, and he is bringing their message out to all the world. Suppose only a few of us are able to see these things; but suppose also they come under the vision of a man like that. Is that not worthwhile? [Applause.] Now, I am not going to talk about recreational needs. I understand it has been assigned to me to talk about the trees. I do not like to be assigned to anything. [Laughter.] There are others who will tell you all about the trees, the many varieties there are, and the reason many varieties are there; and how the West, the East, the North, and the South meet in this wonderful dune country.

What I want to impress on your minds is the beauty and grandeur of this dune country. There are no dunes in America like those over there. The dunes on the various ocean coasts, the dunes that are salt water dunes, are of an entirely different type. They totally lack the poetic inspiration those dunes of Indiana have. The salt sea breezes prevent a great deal of vegetation from growing, and therefore the ocean dunes are not covered with vegetation as ours are. They are not filled with wonderful poetic inspiration as are our dunes. They do not display the wonderful color effect you get these days down in our dunes, such as cannot be found anywhere else in the world. Nowhere else can be found such a wonderful outburst of flora in the spring as is found in our dune woods, when they are covered with a blue sea of wonderful lupin, or phlox, or violets, or many other plants, all wonderful in their color display. Nowhere else can be found such a wonderful expression of spring. The other dunes do not have it. That is why our foreign friends must come to our dunes to find this wonderful poetic expression. They cannot get it at Cape Cod; they cannot find it down in Virginia or in the Carolinas; they cannot find it even on the coasts of France, Holland, or Denmark. There I, as a boy, have often treaded the great dunes that sometimes extended over 16 miles inland, back into the country. But there is nothing of grace or beauty about those dunes. On the contrary, they are a very serious menace indeed, except where the Government has taken measures to prevent them from drifting inland and overwhelming the country. Our dunes are of an entirely different type. They are poetic, they are beautiful, they are wonderful; they are just about the most beautiful and wonderful thing we have in the Middle West.

Only a few days ago I stood on the bluffs of the Mississippi, north of Savannah, and looked up the Mississippi River, with the sun shining on the cornfields of northern Illinois, and below us that mighty river in a deep, mystic mood. It was a wonderful picture, but not nearly as wonderful a picture as I saw in the dunes yesterday, with a group of friends. And, friends, remember one thing: Though we always talk so much about the wonderful national parks of the West, how many of us are ever able to make a pilgrimage to those parks? How many of us? What are we doing for the tens of thousands of people in this noisy, grimy, seething city, who need to revive their souls and refresh the inner man as well as the outer? What are we doing for them? There is only one thing that we can give them, and that is the opportunity to revive their souls in the outglow of beauty from the dunes over yonder on the shores of Lake Michigan. If we should permit that wonderful place to be sold for a "mess of pottage," it would be one of the worst calamities that could befall us. Think of the good Indiana folk. The only outlet they have to Lake Michigan is right there, the only outlet that is left for them. That is the only breathing place they have on the shores of beautiful Lake Michigan, and there is nothing left to the great State of Indiana if that wonderful piece of country is done away with. Now, I am not going to tire you with my remarks any longer. I am just going to say one final word to you, and it is this: That it would be a sad thing, indeed, for this great Central West if this wonderful dune country should be taken away from us and on it built cities like Gary, Indiana Harbor, and others. It would show us to be in fact what we often are accused of being—a people who only have dollars for eyes. We are in duty bound to preserve some of the wild beauty of our country for our descendants. I thank you. [Applause.]

REPORT OF MR. JENS JENSEN, CONSULTING LANDSCAPE ARCHITECT, ON LANDSCAPE DESIGN OF COLUMBUS PARK

Forty-Ninth Annual Report of the West Chicago Park Commissioners,
January 15, 1918

The Honorable, the Board of West Chicago Park Commissioners.

Gentlemen—I beg to submit herewith a brief report setting forth the landscape design of Columbus Park. This new park is approximately square in shape, about one hundred and fifty-four acres in size, and lies on the City limits to the west. One of the problems in its design lay in the fact that an important future business artery, West Harrison street, cuts through the southern portion of this Park. This obstacle was overcome by the closing of that portion of Harrison street within the Park area and by diverting traffic around the southern end of the Park. Another problem lay in the fact that the land acquired consisted of level prairie, with a slight depression at its eastern boundary, caused by one of the ancient lake beaches of pre-historic lake Chicago. This lake terrace is less pronounced here than in many other sections of this region. The difference in elevation is but seven feet.

The motive that guided the landscape plan for Columbus Park is to be found in the general type of landscape in the immediate environment of Chicago. The greater part of the land has been left in its natural form. Water, in the way of a symbolized prairie river, has been introduced at the lower level. At the source of this river, which is in the north central part of the Park, the land has been slightly elevated by filling with excavated material. To the east of the river, an elevation or ridge has been built from the same material. From the southeast section, this ridge skirts along the southern and western boundary of the Park. Along the river, it forms river bluffs, which are an important part of the landscape composition, and serve as a screen to shut out the city to the east. The south ridge conceals a railroad right-of-way which is parallel to the southern boundary of the Park and shuts out the adjacent street.

The object of this is to complete the country vision as far as this is possible within the City.

To give some security to the multitudes that visit the Park on foot, the drives have been constructed close to the border. On the southern boundary, the Park drive merges into the traffic road for which a certain area had to be dedicated as compensation for the vacation of Harrison street. This traffic road is a combination of pleasure driveway and public service road divided from the Park border by the ridge above referred to. This traffic road is really a detour of Harrison street.

The drive in the northern section may be considered a continuation of Jackson boulevard through the Park, following the curved road design rather than the straight lines of the boulevard outside the Park.

Golf and ball fields in the central portion have been left free from walks to avoid accidents. Back of the eastern ridge are the service buildings, outdoor bathing pools, children's playfield, wading pool and tennis courts—all invisible from the interior of the Park. The bathing and swimming pools have been picturesquely designed in accordance with the rock ledges of our Illinois rivers, a laughing brook furnishing water for these pools. A neighborhood house and canoe harbor are located on the turn of the river in the northern part of the park. To the south of the neighborhood house and near the source of the river, is the players' green, dedicated to the drama and to music out-of-doors. This players' green consists of a slightly elevated spot, separated from the space for the audience by a brook. Elm, ash, maple, aspen, hawthornes, crab apples, plums, sumach and hazel, form the decorative material and the setting of the players' green. The brook, fringed with rushes and other water plants, adds to the decorative effect of the green and affords an opportunity for water pageants. The auditorium is a meadow surrounded by a woody ridge. The American drama is still in its making. The writer believes that its early expression will be in the out-of-doors, and he sincerely hopes that this simple but poetic place will become an inspiration that will help to create the great American drama.

Behind the players' green and hidden in the woods, is the council-fire, a gathering place for young and old, but especially for the wood-crafters, Boy Scouts and Camp-Fire Girls.

The narrow strip between the Park drive and the northern boundary of the Park typifies a lane for those who enjoy a quiet walk—such as only a lane of hawthornes, cherries, crabapples, plums, sumach and hazel can give. These and other plants will provide food and nesting places for the birds, whose songs add charm and beauty to a secluded path.

The center of the Park consists of a prairie or large meadow, dedicated to golf and playfields. Several groves of trees break its monotony and furnish shade for the players, at the same time forming the oases in the prairie landscape. The major part of the planting is found on the Park borders, the river bluffs and the elevated section south of the community house. It consists of material native to Illinois, with a large assortment of plants that invite the birds. The ridges are covered with oak, maple, linden, elm, ash, cherry and aspen, with an undergrowth of viburnums, witch hazel, dogwood, chokecherry, Juneberry and plums, and the forest floor is covered with native phlox, trilliums, dogtooth violets and spring beauties, violets, asters, etc. Illinois hawthornes and crabapples are used in great profusion on the woodland border. These more than any other plant of this region express the landscape of northern Illinois, and with their stratified branches give a feeling of breadth and spaciousness, and repeat the horizontal lines of the prairies.

During the Spring, the woodland borders are painted with the colors of hawthornes, crab apples, and plums, with here and there the fleeting note of a red bud. The meadows are fringed with garlands of viburnums, dogwoods and prairie roses. Reflected in the river waters are elm, sycamore, hackberry, birch, water ash, alder, sumach, buttonbush, ninebark, yellow currants, swamp roses, marshmallows, asters and goldenrods, and with a fringe of cat tails, iris, arrow heads, lobelias, calamus, and lilies, phlox and shooting stars, invade the adjoining meadows. The spaces between the drive and the footpath are filled in with such prairie flowers as the coneflower, asters, goldenrods, black-eyed Susans and phlox.

The Autumn days in our Illinois woods are beyond description. Nowhere in the world can be found such a display of colors, such a grand symphony. The winter landscape also has a charm in its various shades of purples, browns, grays and reds, and here again our native material excels in beauty and gives the landscape a character distinctly its own.

But in Columbus Park, our meadow with its woodland borders, our river with its dark shaded bluffs, and our groves with their variation of light and shadow, are only a part of the landscape. The sky above, with its fleeting clouds and its star-lit heavens, is an indispensable part of the whole. Looking west from the river bluffs at sundown across a quiet bit of meadow, one sees the prairie melt away into the stratified clouds above, touched with gold and purple and reflected in the river below. This gives a feeling of breadth and freedom that only the prairie landscape can give to the human soul. Moonlight nights are equally inspiring and are an important part of the landscape composition. On these occasions, from the prairie and the boat landing may be seen the deep shadows of the river bluffs in contrast with the silvery rays of the poetic moon reflected in the waters. What a pity that the matter-of-fact spirit of our day should decree that electric lights must burn in our parks on moonlight nights and thus destroy the beauty and charm of a moonlight evening.

It is evident that first consideration must be given to the aesthetic in our parks—play being at all times subservient. There are multitudes who rarely get beyond the City limits and who obtain a great amount of physical exercise in their daily work but lack mental stimulus. They need the out-of-doors, as expressed in beauty and art for a greater vision and a broader interest in life. They need the quietude of the pastoral meadow and the soothing green and woodland in contrast with the noise and glare of the great city. They need the things that bring joy and beauty into their souls and give them a fuller enjoyment of life. Should this not be told them in the language of their native landscape, so that they may here experience our native beauty, and thus not be deprived of the opportunity to commune with Nature even though it be in very small measure? Should we not learn to love the things amidst which we have built our homes? And are not these things essential to full expression of a higher and better life to each and every one?

A GREATER WEST PARK SYSTEM

West Park Commission Report, 1920

THE REASON FOR THE PLAN

After going back fifty years to the time when our present park system was born, we realize more and more the great vision in the minds of the far-sighted men of that day. Chicago then, with less than four hundred thousand inhabitants, undertook to carry out a plan, which for size and expenditure in relation to the wealth of the city, certainly must have our sincere respect and admiration. It took great courage and imagination to formulate and carry it through successfully. The pioneers of yesterday have passed. Are the pioneers of today equal to the task?

At the time of its conception, the present park system was situated in the outskirts of the city, quite remote from the densely populated sections. Today miles of thickly settled areas have grown up beyond the park system, without any provision whatever for parks and playgrounds. We now have a city of three million inhabitants, and more than one million two hundred thousand of these reside on the west side. With the exception of our modern playgrounds and of Columbus Park, now under construction, nothing has been added to the original park areas projected in 1869. And besides these great park areas, the grown-ups and children of those earlier days had thousands of acres of open prairies for breathing spaces and playgrounds. But the city has spread so that these former vacant lands are now subdivision after subdivision of dwelling houses and factory sites.

At the present time, the entire park lands for the one million, two hundred thousand people of the west side comprise only seven hundred and sixty-five acres, with forty-three additional acres of playgrounds. Account also must be taken of the fact that the great mass of citizens living west of the river are not favored with large worldly possessions. They have little or no means to travel or to spend their vacations in the Michigan or Wisconsin woods, and still less to visit our National Parks. Many indeed cannot even afford to spend the week ends in our forest preserves. These are the people who keep industry and commerce moving. Both their and their children's requirements in healthy recreation are supremely important to the future development of the city.

More parks mean health to a greater number of people. Parks consist of growing things, quite the opposite of dust-producing streets and alleys and the unhealthy fumes and gases from shops and factories. When we realize how the present style in city buildings, particularly as it is on the north side, where the buildings crowd against each other with their front walls extending to the edge of the sidewalk, keeps the air and light from human beings and all plant life, then we shall understand the great necessity for more green spaces in the City Complex. Parks mean a spreading out of the building areas. They mean the country close at hand. These green wedges are the greatest distributors of health and beauty in our modern city, for it is always a better city where the perfumes of blossoms and the sweetness of growing things blow in through the open windows. To come in contact with living plants is an inspiration to the mind that brings the body well-being and content. It is a new world for the city-bred that broadens out his vision and makes him better fitted for the struggle of existence.

Over-crowding the parks means a constant deterioration of the lawn and planting areas, and hence results in a high cost of maintenance. Well-kept parks will take care of only a certain number of visitors. When parks are overcrowded, and their beauty is marred by worn-out lawns and decaying trees, the general public loses respect and appreciation for them as recreation centers, and shows this by its indifference to park rules, as, for example, by making numerous paths across the grass and by destroying flowering plants. Thus the parks' real service to the community is lost. And from the viewpoint of art, by which their value must also be measured, their standards are lowered to mediocrity. Neatness in park maintenance is a most essential thing, and it is impossible to achieve this in an over-crowded park.

Well-maintained parks afford, too, a great deal of instruction in out-door beauty, which sooner or later is revealed in the parkways and backyards of the residents of the surrounding district. This is an influence whose value for greater civic beauty cannot be overestimated.

The forest preserves, now being acquired, can never provide the multitudes, who today are spreading over the prairies of the west side, with sufficient park space. They are too remote to be within easy reach of the great mass of people living west of our present park system. The author remembers quite well the almost impossible task he and his family experienced in reaching a park three or four miles distant on a holiday a good many years ago. At that time, moreover, the west side had less than half the population it has to-day, and the cars were not so crowded. In thickly settled districts, no home should be more than two miles away from some park. The shorter the distance, the larger the number of people who will visit it and be benefitted by it. In fact a walking distance is the most satisfactory. The forest preserves are to give us the beauty and inspiration that are inherent in our native woods. They should remain a bit of primitive Illinois. Furthermore, overcrowding the forest preserves will ultimately mean their destruction, too.

History

. . . The acquisition of these historic lands for park purposes will add a new sentiment to the parks, and the preservation of memorable spots in our early history will be made secure. The history of the past will be linked up with that of today, and interest in the old history of our region is bound to grow as the distance from those days becomes greater. The placing of commemorative tablets would tell the particular historic interest of this region to all park visitors. . . .

The Sterling Morton High School and the Goodwin Grammar School, both situated on the east side of Austin Avenue, should be incorporated in the scheme and surrounded by a playground and parking in harmony with the general plan. On Street 16 or Street 17, either equally serviceable for this purpose, a connection is proposed with Ridge Road and Gage Farm, and extended thence to the Forest Preserves along the Des Plaines River and Salt Creek, and to join with the contemplated Zoological Garden. South of Columbus Park the boulevard crosses Roosevelt Road, which is to follow the Illinois Valley, and which will form a direct connecting link between Chicago and St. Louis. . . . From the Chicago, Burlington and Quincy tracks south, the country is practically open, and at the present writing is used for farming and truck gardening. Here the author recommends the securing of a strip of from 800 to 1,000 feet in width, that will permit spaces for recreation and play. From Columbus Park south the plan proposes a winding road. On the wider area mentioned before, a curved road is easily adapted, and is preferable to a straight one. Its merging into the proposed Park at the terminal of Austin Avenue between the south branch of the Chicago River and the Drainage Canal will not be noticeable. This park should have not less than seven or eight hundred acres. Some of the lands here are low and hence well adapted to a water-landscape of considerable dimensions. This lagoon should be connected with the Chicago River and through the old Ogden ditch with the Des Plaines River. A driveway should follow the river to the Des Plaines River and here connect by driveway with the Forest Preserves at Mount Forest and Palos Park. Another connection could also be made with the Drainage Canal, if this should become desirable. From this park on the east, the belt follows the south branch of the Chicago River with a width, including both banks of the river, of not less than three to four hundred feet. At proper intervals this width is to be increased to a thousand or more feet, for small parks and municipal truck gardens. A larger park is suggested at 52nd. . . .

CONCLUSION

The present day tendency, whether we like it or not, is strongly for the crowded urban life. The immigrant, especially the one who comes from southern Europe, and the boy and the girl from the farm, all flock to the city, and particularly to the great commercial and industrial centers, such as Chicago. Then, too, speculations in real estate, poorly considered building laws and laxity of proper building supervision, and questionable politics further increase the crowding and congestion in city construction. The result is, in many districts, intolerable conditions for human habitation, and these cheerless, congested areas become breeding grounds of vice and criminality where the sense of civic responsibility becomes nullified, and the mob spirit easily gains ascendancy.

To better this congested condition is one of the chief problems of our age. That the proposed plan will solve all the evil influences of city life, the author does not for a moment think, but that it will reduce many of the evils to a minimum he does believe. Making all individuals understand and appreciate the value of beautiful surroundings, if it is not within them to do so, is of course impossible; but, allowed a decent home environment, a respect for neatness and beautiful things is given a chance to grow in a community, and the result will be that from year to year there will be an increase in the numbers of those who will appreciate a better life for both their own good and for that of their descendants. This in the course of time might create a yearning for home gardens—each home with its own garden in which a part of the leisure hours may be put to good results, both morally and physically. To own a bit of native soil is the backbone and the security of our democracy.

We know that trees are cool and comforting in summer, and that they reduce the hot glariness of building walls and street pavements, that they soften the stiff hard lines of architecture, and generally add beauty to the city street, and we do not question that growing things are better than cinders in the garden, nor that the message the little flower brings is of the sweetest, noblest kind. But more attention must be given to the real value of growing things. If a tree is planted, security must be provided that it will grow if given the proper care. A soil filled with foul gases, and an air full of poisonous fumes are deathly to both human and vegetable life. Where trees can live, human life will thrive. Parks and playgrounds offer a place for wholesome sport and social pleasure, and a place of rest and quiet from the noisy street.

This, however, is only one phase of city building. To surround each home with a garden must be the final solution of urban life.

Altogether we see in this park plan a more beautiful city; a city whose buildings are interspersed with growing things,—trees, shrubs and flowers,—and whose streets are broken by playgrounds and broad stretches of woodlands and meadows; a city that is a fairer world for the city dweller to live in. New interests will be added to his life and his vision will be broadened and extended beyond the narrow confines of his city walls. Sunshine will no longer be at a premium, and sound bodies and happy minds will be a consequence. The cost can never be too great. We have no right to consider ourselves civilized as long as we permit less fortunate residents of our city to live and multiply in unhealthy surroundings that are devoid of beauty and that are a peril to the whole population, and a menace to the normal development of our civilization. There are those among us for whom the rural influences in the city complex are essential to their very existence. This is well to keep in mind in our future city building, if we desire to prevent from degeneration and eventual extermination some of the sturdiest and noble peoples who have come to our shore.

Unsatisfactory city conditions drive the more fortunate in worldly goods to the building of suburban communities. This is a distinct loss to the city. Usually, men and women of great worth are amongst those who migrate to the suburbs. Those who need to remain in the struggle where they are confronted with the needs and wants of the city every day of their life, and thus are better fitted to lend their effort and influence to improve the physical and moral life of the city. The average suburban town or village does not present the normal life which is found in a self-sustaining community. Consequently has not the problems to solve of the latter. It is a poor city that drives its people away, and into the suburbs. Both the urbanite and suburbanite suffer by this transaction. To make the modern city liveable is the task of our times. If this plan as presented here can help to make life better and more beautiful, it serves its purpose well.

I LIKE OUR PRAIRIE LANDSCAPE

The Park International, July 1920

My first impression of the prairie country was of its richness in flowers. It was one grand carpet of exquisite colors such as is fit for a Forest Cathedral, and such as nature only knows how to weave. Some of the color expressions were as dramatic as the afterglow of the setting sun. And above this carpet, like a flare of trumpets, rose the hawthorn and the western crabapple—the hawthorn garlanded with myriads of white roses, and the crabapple painting the edge of the prairie with its delicate virgin pink. Only on a flat, level plain is it possible to notice the character and beauty of these small trees. Strong and daring, with a feeling of freedom and nobility, they lift their heads above the surface of the land. They are always the first to greet us, and they are interesting and beautiful at all seasons of the year whether in flower, in leaf or in fruit. In winter, the bare, gray, outstretched branches of the hawthorn, that symbolize the horizontal lines of the prairie, light up the purple borders of the forest, and the violet branches of the crabapple, playing in the different lights of the day, add a poetic charm to the woodlands, and especially to the purple ridges of oaks— those centuries old monarchs of noble birth.

These were my first impressions. As years have passed by, they have grown both in number and in depth. There is no season of the year that this Illinois landscape does not possess its charm for me. At times it has intimate notes of great delicacy. One early spring, strolling through a bit of woods that were but a ruin of their former grandeur, I met a group of gray dogwood showing the first signs of life. The delicate rose of their sprouting buds put a refinement into these scarred and despoiled woods that brought back some of their primitive wealth. Nearby a gray haw, with lace-like branches wove itself into the dark timber of the decaying trees. It was refreshing to find these slender notes here where all was tragedy, and what a promise they gave for the future. There is a tenderness in the deciduous forest that the conifer forest does not possess. One realizes this when one passes through the dividing line of the Wisconsin woods and the Illinois woods.

I used to wonder why our parks and gardens were so poor in their fall colors, but gradually I came to understand that it was because they were in discord with the native landscape. With their foreign plants, they were nothing but out-of-doors museums; they represented a conglomeration of things purchased over the counter. Except for a few plants, their growing things had no coloring, or were not ripe for the change of foliage when the first frost threw it withered to the ground. They were an importation, unfitted to meet the struggle for life here, and hence doomed to destruction. Their expression was material, not spiritual; one of possession rather than of art. They did not belong. They were not what the Great Master had meant for this place.

If America shall ever pride itself for any art of its own, that art must grow out of the native soil. We shall never receive credit for things that we steal or copy from others. Landscape gardening is the one art that is dependent upon soil and climatic conditions. How can it ever become native and thrive if we have utter disregard for the materials of which it is composed? Those gardens that have survived in ancient Europe grew out of materials that gave that particular section of the country its character and its charm. So must ours, if we are ever to build parks and gardens which express the best that our country can give.

However, there will never be only one type of American landscape gardening, but there will be as many types as there are differences in climate and differences in topographical character of the various sections. How wonderfully rich then will this country become, when the noble art of landscape gardening has been fully understood and appreciated by our people; when each section of our great land has developed the thing that fits it best! For each section has a soul of its own, a beauty of its own. Eventually there will be eyes born to see the truth.

For me, I like our Illinois landscape best. Deep down through its rich prairie land, during countless ages, the river has cut its winding path in water-worn canyons, bordered by woody bluffs and lofty cliffs. This is the garden of the prairie country, a motive for landscape art, full of imagination, mystery and poetic charm—a hidden garden, as it were, in the broad expanse of the prairie landscape. Interesting by contrast with each other, both have a spiritual value and give a wonderful vision. The one is romantic, lovely and intimate in its finer expressions, while the other breathes breadth and freedom. There is nothing in the out-of-doors that excels this landscape. Here are shadowy nooks and sunlit fields, singing waters and rustling leaves. In the streams fish play hide-and-seek with the rushes and water nymphs, and one hears the splash of a leaping bass. Over the meadows, butterflies flit from flower to flower to the song of the meadow lark. It is a sanctuary, a cathedral in the out-of-doors.

From the towering bluffs, one gets the full significance of the free and spreading prairies. Just now they are dotted with great bouquets of apple blossoms. There are shady lanes where the birds may nest and thrill the wanderer with their lovely song, and there are broad stretches of flowers, a symbol of the prairie that has passed.

Here is a grove of western crabapple, carpeted with violets, and there a knoll of birch and Juneberries, carpeted with hepaticas. There are colonies of native plum, bride of early spring, amongst the lovely bluebells. There are secret groves of white oaks in their spring dress of silver and rose, and with their golden tassels shining in the sun.

I am looking into this landscape now. The spring is in its making—a shimmering green like a mysterious mist is visible. Nowhere in the world is the meaning of the returning sun so forceful as in this deciduous forest of the north. No landscape is richer in poetic expression, none more tender and refined in color and form. To desecrate such a shrine is vandalism. On its purity and nobility will eventually be founded a great American art.

WISCONSIN BEAUTIFUL

The Country Magazine, May 1921

I still remember vividly my first trip to the Dalles of the Wisconsin River. This was back in the nineties and before the time when the Dalles had lost one of their greatest charms, the roaring of the waters through the narrows. For one who has spent his life on the prairies, this contrast between the precipitous cliffs and the deep canyons of the Wisconsin and the broad and level prairies was quite a revelation, in fact, that the imprints left upon my mind will remain there. I never have visited the Dalles since, and I do not expect to be there again, because their greatest charm has been destroyed by commercial greed.

The Devil's Lake country was as great a revelation to me some years later. I can still see the lofty cliffs as we approached the lake from the south—like mountains in their purple cloaks they loomed out of the mysterious waters. It was a new experience so much different from the river scenery of Wisconsin and of our own Illinois and Rock Rivers.

One day I read in the Chicago Herald an advertisement from a hotel at Beaver Lake. The name sounded wild and rustic to me and I surely expected to see a real beaver at work. A few days later I set out to find it, and to my surprise, it was an extremely tame and cultivated region but never-the-less of charming landscape and for more than fourteen years, sometimes several times during the summer, Beaver Lake and the surrounding country as far north as Holy Hill was paid a visit. Sometimes it was a pilgrimage to see the sun rise, but more often to see the sun set over the purple ridges far to the west. Even now I long for another view from Holy Hill, and I know of no place with a view of more intimate charm and greater poetic expression.

The northern woods with their thousand lakes and many hidden brooks came last and are still a mystery to me. Perhaps they will always remain so. I have wandered amongst the trailing arbutus when the forest was filled with their sweet perfume and when millions of catkins on the northern alders transformed the forest into a tracery of the most delicate pattern. I have felt the solemnity of the noble pines—the cathedral of the out-of-doors and prayed that just one—one noble giant forest might be spared to give its great message to those who follow us. It was my great privilege last November to receive an impression of the northern landscape not to be forgotten. Just as we were skirting the hills north of Sturgeon Bay, a ridge covered with birch and beech loomed up in the back-ground in the most delicate shades of rose and grey a great symphony as it were. This will always be remembered by me as one of the sweetest notes in the northern landscape.

I do not want to minimize the impressions of my first journey to Door county, especially those gained as we turned down the cliffs at Fish Creek far above the jagged shore line now illuminated by the afterglow of the setting sun and below the indigo blue waters of Green Bay. What I saw on that first visit drew me close to Door county, and I have become better acquainted, particularly with its northern part. Many mornings I have seen the Ellison Bay cliffs painted rosy by the dawn, and again at dusk I have seen them in their deep purples rising out of the sea like some mysterious phantom land. And what an inspiration to stand at Death's Door and watch the Northern Lights play. These rocks have withstood, for countless ages, the fury of the storm and the rushing of the waters, as they eternally pound against the rocky precipices. Here they have stood since the dawn of things, and if man leaves them untouched, here they will remain far into the unknown tomorrow, inspiring those who understand their purpose and teaching to others their message. They are among Wisconsin's greatest treasures.

It is now my great pleasure, for a part of every year, to sit on the cliffs of Green Bay and watch the sun disappearing over the purple ridges far to the west in Upper Michigan. There I can watch the illumination of the setting sun as it plays its wonderful color symphony on the blue waters of the bay. It is my hope that these cliffs and the rugged river bluffs and the lake shore will remain unspoiled so that the generations to come may enjoy them and be inspired by them for the betterment of themselves and of their race. Surely a love for the native soil must grow and thrive amongst the hills and lakes of Wisconsin.

LANDSCAPE GARDENING— AN ART

Gartenschöenheit, April 1923

Ever so often one of Dr. Heggeman's observations goes through my mind which he made during his visit here. Years have passed since then. It was on a beautiful winter's day. We were crossing the open countryside near the woodlands along the Des Plaines River, when he asked me to stop the car so that he could fully appreciate the magic of the colors in our woodlands in winter, as they became visible beyond the pastures. After he had asked me for the names of the various trees and plants which made up this color composition, he spoke these remarkable words: "In Germany we have only very few of our original woodlands left; most of our woods have been re-forested and now have a value of so and so many Marks. Don't you believe that if we had retained such richness of color in our woodlands that we could hope that something noble and great could still sprout from the German soil?" Again and again I have repeated these words during public speeches, because they are not just highly significant for us here in America, but far more so for you in old Europe.

Today I am surrounded by the same splendor of color that Dr. Heggeman saw. It seems so radiant, so full of music and poetry, such a cheerful accord that mere mortals like us are hardly capable to do justice to them, let alone try to express them with our pitiful attempts at landscape painting. Opposite me is a very different garden, a garden with the stamp of dollars and cents upon it; it belongs to a collector who does not understand anything about art, but who loves the diversity and the accumulation of things, especially those things that attract the visitor's attention. It is a conglomerate of differences; each one of them sings its own melody in shrill disharmony, not at all like the symphony that the woodlands around me are singing, but like an open air museum that is standing in the pointed light of a domineering class consciousness in competition with its similarly disposed neighbors. True art does not know competition; love predominates instead.

I do not quarrel with this picture because I do not have to look at it, because it is up to me to close my eyes when I pass by or to look to the other side where the landscape is full of grace and beauty. But I would like to figure out whether landscape gardening or landscape architecture belongs to the fine arts which is measured according to the same rules as a beautiful poem or a musical composition, or whether it is only a trade. And I have come to the conclusion that there can be no mention of art as long as the creator of a landscape is being guided by the principle of diversity and the collection of novelties—be it for scientific reasons or to simply outdo a neighbor—rather than by love, beauty and an inner happiness that is to radiate from the picture.

You may call it narrow-minded or petty to try to create a landscape picture from native plants only, but you should remember that we grew up among these plants, that they continually taught us a special idiom since the infancy of our tribe, that they are woven into the soul of our race and—in truth, no art of landscape gardening can be called true art that can reflect the soul of a tribe, if it does not borrow its tools of expression from the surroundings that are necessary for the survival of the people. This is the only way in which it possible to fill the world with cheerful delight in which everyone creates the best in his own particular way with his very own materials and the talents that are lying dormant in him. This is what I consider the true height of civilization. Once you can speak your own language, you are ready to learn the language of other people, if you so desire; but first learn your mother tongue! Once you know yourself well, then you will be able to understand and honor other people and allow them the freedom to live their lives according to their own discretion. There would never have been a Beethoven, if the musical notes with which he composed his glorious music, would have been chosen by him according to the desire for novelty and diversity of material, or would have been put together from a catalogue. His music flowed from his creative soul, just like every other genuine work of art. It has to flow freely and unfettered from the soul of the artist, no matter where he lives: It should be like a sweet folk tune—which true gardens are like—free of any ulterior motive of ownership and of flaunting wealth, this source of arrogance and intolerance, of hate and jealousy. True love of the beauty of the whole is the basis of creating a garden and not the scientific knowledge of the individual living being. The spirit of such a garden is the spirit of democracy, the spirit of a new day; it means to honor the simplest things in life, and those that grow to a ripe old age, while rooted in the earth of home, free and untamed by the hands of man. I say free from human influence because every fully developed plant has its own beauty and its individual habit which it should be allowed to develop. I am convinced that these are the tasks of landscape gardening.

But do not misunderstand me: I am not talking of raising fruit and vegetables, nor of the economic side of horticulture, for which production has to be the overriding principle. I am talking of the soft touch of the world of color, that something which rings throughout our whole home, our house and our whole self. Unfortunately we poor city dwellers are usually not conscious of it, we may not even own a plant; but here the community has to take the place of the individual and has to express the art of landscape gardening in its parks and gardens. Nonetheless there will always be men and women who own more wealth and land on this earth to add a small park to their house—something that we should all be entitled to whether we have the means or not.

Let us also remember that with an expanding population, with the continual growth of our cities the original form of our landscape—all that gives the land its distinctive character—is slowly disappearing and slipping away from the grasp of ever broader strata of the population. We cannot attain a healthy and normal civilization without a certain influence from the original, the prehistoric soil, in which we are all rooted which is a part of our selves and always should remain so. This is necessary here in America, but it is even more necessary for you in Europe and especially so in those cities of culture which suffer from root-rot. There may be glory and power in the showing off of great wealth, but life within more modest guidelines is safer and in the last resort also more fertile. The art of a people will demonstrate whether its soul is healthy or not. The same applies to gardens: in a certain sense they reflect the cultural life of a people; and happy is the nation that does not forget its simple folk tunes, nor the native hazelnut along the roadside. There is more loveliness, more beauty, more trust and more love in those things that belong to us all than in the exotic tree—however beautiful it may be—in the garden of the rich man showing off his belongings. His soul is often untouched by true beauty and he resembles a collector of pictures who cares more for their financial than their artistic value.

Some years ago I came across the home of a poor fisherman in a newly developed area of Wisconsin. From the distance I noticed a radiant spot of color in front of the window of the little log cabin. The house was located beautifully under the sheltering branches of sugar maple and beech, an attractive combination which is thoroughly natural, yet they had been selected in a such way that it looked as if the fisherman had left them untouched out of reverence for the trees. As I approached I saw that the radiant spot of color was a group of hollyhock—just imagine hollyhock—whose roots he had received from a dear friend, long since passed away. It is a rough country where this fisherman has made his home and we can imagine the longing with which this family is looking forward toward the awakening of spring, when the snow finally melts after 6 months and the first signs of life appear on the hollyhock. Then the period of waiting full of longing when the shoots grow past the window sill and further past the window and then the general jubilation when one day a member of the family discovers the first flower looking in through the window to announce its gentle message! They only have this one clump of hollyhock, that is their entire garden, that is all they need. It is worth more to this fisherman's family than all the gardens of the rich people all over the world: it is the only garden worth caring for;

it speaks its wonderful language to them all the time, even in winter when they savor the awakening of spring in advance. It is a folk tune, a poem, and it touches their soul. One day—or so I hope—everyone will own a garden like this, a garden he loves and who returns this love and sings the most beautiful melody ever sung. Only good people live in such a garden.

Translation from the German "Die Landschaftsgäertnerei—eine Kunst," by Margarete R. Harvey, ASLA

ROADSIDE PLANTING

Landscape Architecture, April 1924

Roadside planting should be a part of the general character of the landscape so that the roads themselves do not appear as a definite line apart from the rest of the scenery, but a means to an end that is in sympathy with its surroundings. The highways are the points from which the traveler sees and enjoys the surrounding country. It is therefore of importance that the roadside planting should not shut out adjacent lands. Out on the plains, the open country and the freedom of it is a real charm and inspiration. Even roadsides lined with rows of trees in the avenue fashion would be a mistake. This not only would change the broad expanse of prairie country, but would tend to checkerboard the prairie landscape. The same disadvantage would exist also in mountainous countries, where the continuity of the valley is the object of beauty.

Scattered trees planted promiscuously along the highway, as one sees them in the forest, are more in keeping with our landscape and with the American mind than the stately avenues of monarchies. It is rather lanes that we want, or "pikes," as they are called in the South, where trees seem to enjoy the roadside and each other's company. There is nothing stiff or set about it. A lane or a pike is tolerant even to the shy but sweet violet that may be permitted to scatter its perfume along the highway. I have seen pikes in Kentucky that come as near to what I consider a beautiful American highway as anything I know of. They are serviceable, beautiful, and cool on hot summer days. Native plants of all sorts find a happy home along these roadsides and give their beauty and their wonderful message to the passerby, and in them nest our birds that thrill us with their songs.

We want this expression of freedom along the open road. We want shadows and we want sunlight. We want the comfort of shady lanes and we want the beautiful outlooks over the surrounding country.

All roadside planting should be determined and based on the country and its native vegetation through which the road winds its way. In this way the roadside planting will become a part of the general landscape and enhance the beauty of its surroundings as far as this is possible for a highway to do. For instance, swamp and lowland landscapes are of a widely different character from prairie or hilly country and the vegetations fitting for these different types of landscapes are equally different.

Never have I seen a white oak finer and the landscape nobler by the oak being a part of it, than on one beautiful May day in Missouri with the oak crowned with golden tassels against the blue sky. This is just one instance where the oak or any other tree will bring out its greatest beauty when planted in a fitting situation. Every plant has its proper place in the out-of-doors. To find this place is worthwhile, because here it reveals its greatest beauty and gives us joy in the fullest measure. Trees adapted to their environs may grow to great age and nobility and in this way highway planting will become a most important task in the making of our rural landscapes. This points to another important matter—the designing and supervision of the work. It is a matter of great importance, a matter that requires great knowledge of plant life as well as the vision of the artist.

Roadside planting, the development of state reservations, and rural parks are equal in importance to city planning and are far greater in scope and vision than the latter. A period of great cultural advancement is always measured by the vision and the outlook for the future. Roadside planting belongs to such a period. It is pioneer work with us, but it is a part, and a very important part, of a great cultural movement of our people.

NOVELTY VERSUS NATURE

Landscape Architecture, October 1924

On my daily trip to Ravinia, I have to pass a street in one of our suburban villages that until lately bordered on a bit of primitive woods, a remnant of the great elm forest that once covered this region. Slowly home after home has crept into these woods and little by little the forest has vanished, but the spirit of it has been preserved by most home owners leaving the old trees wherever it was possible to do so. The last remnant of the forest that was remained for a prominent architect to slaughter. Trees hundreds of years old, amongst which every American should have been proud to build his home, seeking comfort and beauty under their leafy shade, are now piled up in cord wood. The lovely carpet of beautiful flowers that greeted us in the spring has gone. This might be expected, as few have given ample study to the practical utilization of the forest flora. But what about the trees? During our semi-tropical summers, we need the coolness of leafy shade, and we also need—what is far more important—the message of century-old trees, their nobility and history. They link us back to pioneer life; they teach us the beauty of our native country; they enrich our love for native soil, and they are woven into our cultural life.

This is what happened. The beauty that was has been scrapped for novelties. I know only too well that we are living in the age of novelties and good salesmanship. Art is little recognized and less understood. Magnificent native trees were felled to make room for horticultural novelties. Here the red maple had greeted us with its bright flowers in early spring, as it greeted me in the Cumberland hills not long ago,—as it were, a stroke of the Master's brush against mountain slope. Its tiny red leaves glittering in the spring sun with the brilliancy of the last rays of sunset will never return. Neither will its lovely summer foliage, cool and inviting, followed by flaming colors in autumn. And even in winter, its silvery branches illuminate the forest and our dark winter days. What would our northern landscape be with the maple trees out of it?

I bow my head in shame—to the ignorance of a great architect who planted a Schwedler maple on the grave of a noble red maple. A Schwedler maple of fall coloring in spring and rusty green during summer! A Schwedler maple—a mere horticultural novelty.

AMERICAN GARDEN THOUGHTS

Gartenschöenheit, August 1925

. . . The Americans—and I mean the people in general—have a simple taste. I have seen their cities from Maine to the Rocky Mountains. They love the wide, green lawns and they like trees because of the shade. At least the men do; the mothers may wish for a few more bunches of flowers, maybe even a branch of lilac for the heart, or a flowering shrub from the woods, but green is the dominant color; and every now and then some vegetables, especially on the farms. All of it depends on the amount of work the owner wants to invest in it. He wants to have time for other things than horticulture, because it is not a matter of economics for him. He can afford to buy his vegetables, even a bunch of cut flowers, if he so desires. Otherwise he does not like it when everything is dolled up too much, and that is the main difference between us and Europe. And it will always be so.

There is openness and freedom in our gardens. The streets in villages and cities demonstrate it. Any mutilation (pruning) of the vegetation goes against the grain of the genuine American. We love our freedom, and this freedom will be expressed in our gardens despite the constant introduction of European ideas. Apart from what I just described, you will find a few pots or metal containers full of pelargonium, fuchsia, geranium, or an occasional begonia of the toughest variety in the porch or on a bench built into a wall. The ambitious owner will have a group of hollyhocks, phlox or tiger lilies in his front yard, or maybe one or two peonies, maybe even a climbing rose on the wall. This is the average garden in the United States.

Yet I forget the elm and the sugar maple. If the pioneer's home is in the forest, he might have chosen the site for his log cabin below a stately native tree. This pioneer garden will be expanded by a few shrubs or trees depending on the size of the lot, and maybe a few groups of flowers may be added, however, the green grass is the most important. Nothing must be done to damage or detract from its size.

Every now and then the emotions play a role in the garden. Not long ago somebody showed me a 200 year old lilac. It had been moved to Indiana from the former home in Pennsylvania where it was planted by a Dutch immigrant.

This is the typical garden of the majority in the United States. It will stay like this into the distant future. European influences cannot change it. Customs and traditions, influenced by climatic and economic conditions, will guarantee it. But in this simplicity there is great beauty and wholesomeness.

Translation from the German "Amerikanische Gartengedanken," by Margarete R. Harvey, ASLA

THE PARK POLICY

A Park and Forest Policy for Illinois, 1926

To most persons Illinois is a prairie state, but to those who are acquainted with its landscape as a whole, Illinois has varied aspects. It has many prairies, it is true,—rich lands that are yellow with ripening corn in autumn, and it has great marshes along its slow-moving rivers, but it also has rock formations through which, during the ages, the streams of Illinois have cut deep, forming picturesque crags, canyons and bluffs. In the South is the Ozark uplift, a rugged, rocky country with outstanding ridges that are locally known as mountains. And along the Rock, the Illinois, and the Mississippi rivers are peculiar rock formations that are rich in Indian lore.

Most of the soil of Illinois is tillable and should of course be used for agriculture, for fertile land must serve mankind by growing food. Some areas are naturally suited to forestry; in the extreme Southern part there are sections, both large and small, covered with cypress and yellow pine, and in the Northern part are found tamarack and white cedar, and there are small forested areas here and there over the whole state.

The scenic areas, the spots that have beauty without crop fertility, are needed for state parks and should be so preserved. Occasionally, also, when the museum value, so to speak, of a wooded area is greater than its lumber value, it should be preserved as a park rather than as a forest. An instance of this kind is the White Pine Forest of Ogle County which was made into a state park by act of the Legislature several years ago. This is the only stand of white pine left in Illinois and thus is immeasurably valuable as a natural museum.

These park sites should be kept in their native state. For the object of the park reservations is to preserve the scenic beauty of Illinois in its primitive form and to hold it as an heritage for generations yet unborn. There is an inherent quality of great force in primitive beauty that is invaluable to mankind. The primitive world is a different world from the man-made one; it is the work of the Great Master. It is youth, ever renewing itself. And it is only when an artist tries to interpret the message of the primitive world that great art is born. If we would produce great artists and great thinkers we must keep beautiful bits of landscape untouched by "improvements." Moreover, not only artists need this primitive world; we all need the spiritual influence close contact with it gives us. We can get that spiritual influence in no human made thing.

Consequently, these park reservations should be held as free from man-made reminders as is possible. They should not have dance pavilions or merry-go-rounds. These things belong in the city and the village; they are out of place in reservations that are dedicated to nature's beauty. There should be sociability in the parks, but it should be the sociability of gathering around the open fire or dancing on a natural meadow. We go to nature to get a different kind of recreation than we can get in built-up areas, and we must not confuse the two.

Reservations should be located so as to be accessible to all the people of the state. However, nature more or less controls the selection through its distribution of the picturesque. But now good roads and our fast moving vehicles shorten distance so that, in a sense, location is not of such great importance any longer.

State reservations should be selected by an appointed board or a committee of men with technical qualifications for this task. There are several methods by which the land can be secured: through legislation; by purchase; by condemnation; by donation or gift; by easement.

No State reservation or park should be less than one thousand acres in area. The larger the tract, the better it will give the spirit of the wilderness. The counties should take care of the smaller areas under the Forest Preserve Law.

A well designed system of roads should connect all State parks and the main arteries of through highways. As these roads are dedicated more to pleasure, they should not have the straight line or the most direct way as the chief objective of their planning; rather, beauty should rule, and they should go through the most beautiful parts of the state, through both scenic areas and prosperous farming country. They should be located over existing roads, insofar as this is possible, and heavy freight carriers should be debarred from them, if feasible. The roadsides should be planted with plants indigenous to the region, in a way not to hide the adjoining country or to destroy the spirit of the open, as we find it here on the plains. Roads should lead to the reservations from different points, and no roads should be built on the reservations. Railroads as passenger carriers are of secondary value, but it may be found desirable, especially on reservations far from great centers of population, to use railroads as a means to reach them.

Trails should lead into and through the reservations and to interesting points. Each trail should be properly marked at its beginning and end, at the intersection of other trails, and at points of special scientific or historic interest.

At each entrance to the reservation, a properly constructed parking place with water and adequate sanitary facilities must be provided and must be service-able in all kinds of weather. The construction of these general parking spaces should not interfere with or destroy wooded tracts of the reservation.

Campsites must be provided, but they should be located on the outskirts only, in spaces left open by nature, and they should be near to the roads. There should be two kinds of camps, one for transients, and one of a more permanent type. In order to prevent overcrowding, not more than twelve tents should be allowed in a camp, and every camp should be provided with proper water and sanitary arrangements and sufficient parking space. It should also have several outdoor cooking places, a simple shelter for laundry, and a council fire for gatherings of groups in camp.

Roads leading to these campsites should be of the logging type. By this is meant a road, not macadamized, but laid with stone or gravel in the wheel tracks, leaving the grass and other growing plants between the tracks.

No concessions should be permitted on the reservation, and no buildings erected except those necessary for camp life.

No quarrying, mining, or excavating for gravel or sand should be permitted on the reservation. Such materials of this nature as are needed for the reservation should be brought from lands adjacent to but not within the boundaries of the park. Nor should waterpower operations be permitted on the reservations.

The maintenance of the reservations should be by State taxation. The maintenance should be of the simplest kind—keeping the parking and camping places clean and in good repair, replanting areas that have been destroyed by fire, and replanting cut-over lands that have become a part of the reservation on account of their rugged character. All replanting should be done with material indigenous to the region; no foreign plants should be introduced. No live material of any kind should be cut or removed, nor should dead trees, except where a section of the reservation has been destroyed by fire or storm. A dead tree may eventually become a world of interest in itself when covered with mosses, fungi, and other plants that soon find a home in the decaying trunk.

The reservation at all times should have proper fire and police patrol, and should be managed by a warden thoroughly familiar with and trained in arborculture and the natural sciences.

NATURE THE SOURCE

The Vista, Spring 1927

If the city gives in full measure of all that is required to an intellectual life, why seek the country or the primitive wilderness for a change in thoughts and life? Man is an inseparable part of the whole creation—the sea, the mountains, the forest, the streams, the hills, the valleys and its wild life. When man has scorned the cultural value of the out-of-doors, his mental and physical power has been on the decline.

Great minds are a result of close contact with the world not of our making. It is a contact with the Master's Work. A people that understands this and appreciates it fully persist intellectually and physically. I repeat—It is in God's free air that great minds grow. The thing that impresses us most and has the greatest influence on our life is our immediate surroundings, the things we grow up with—whether this be city, town, or country. In the country the variety of things that plays on our imagination is far greater than in the city—there is more real depth; more mystery, especially in the primitive landscape; more food for the mind to play with; the horizon is greater; our thoughts are carried on into the infinite. Look into the unknown depths of the forest or the starry heavens! It is the hills, the brooks, the meadows, the fields and pastures, the woods and the open sea, that we are born among, that we grow up with, and that we finally are laid to rest under, that mean more to us than any other thing outside of our family ties. It is a friendly world. Man's struggle, his hatred, his jealousy, his intolerance seem to step in the silence and reverence of great trees, or in the flower-bedecked meadows in the playing sunlight.

The wild rose of our country inspired McDowell to write his beautiful music composition called "The Wild Rose." Every artist of worth is inspired by the out-of-doors, the Master's creation. It is a message of truth and love that brings only joy and happiness to those who feel its force; and its interpretation is of the highest endeavors and brings out the best in the human soul for the betterment of the race. Native art can only grow out of native soil. It cannot be imported nor purchased with gold. It is that which is our own that we have a right to take pride in, and it is only that which is our own that we shall receive due credit for. Our country is so rich in primitive beauty, so colorful, that it really is a misfortune to those that do not understand it. The deepest patriotism lies in the love for native land and native things, and real accomplishments are an inseparable part of our environments. Time and time again mankind must turn to the primitive where vigor, freshness and youth inspire the mind to renewed action. Heaven save us for the letting down of the intellectual life, due to commercial standardization and efficiency methods that are the main driving wheel in our great commercial age.

For those who practice the art of Landscape Gardening there is only one source for study and it is America as God made it. Its vegetation, its wild life are due to natural selection for fitness for thousands of years. It is fitting and it belongs. To destroy it is to destroy the real America. To corrupt it is the work of stupidity—it is vandalism. One of the most unfortunate things is this changing of the growth that covers our native land, because nothing is more beautiful and more fitting than our native landscape. The beauty of life is to meet its many problems. The joy and the real life of the artist are to solve the various problems in a way harmonious to the environments. There are no greater problems for the Landscape Architect than to try to fit into human habitat those plants best fitted for this purpose, and in harmony with their surroundings. Every plant has a character of its own, and when it is permitted to develop fully will bring beauty and joy—stunted plants are not an art but a craft.

There are two impressions that reached me today, the beginning of spring when everything is pregnant with growth. The first one was the bare silver tops of white oak and sugar maple against a blue sky, with floating gray and lavender clouds. It was a tapestry of the finest weave. It was a color picture of the finest texture. It was Illinois winter landscape at its best. The other impression that inspired me was clouds of pink from the swelling buds of the gray dogwood, and the lacy silver gray of a spreading hawthorn in the dark forest. It expressed the rebirth of life in such a delicate, beautiful way that I know of no other plants that could express it as refined and as touching to the soul. It is such impressions that stir up the emotions and are interpreted in the fine arts. Likewise the silence, the expanse, and the vastness of the prairies fill the human soul with freedom and greatness. Whether it is the musician or the painter, the sculptor or the poet, or any artist, he receives this inspiration from the beginning of things, from the primitive where man's hand has not set its mark, and where the message is pure and direct from the Hand of the Great Maker. Art is the truth. Art is of the spirit.

As a boy I had the habit of walking up a small hill on our farm, from where I could see a rim of purple on the far horizon. In me grew the desire to explore this phantom land, and often I have wondered how much this yearning that grew in me from year to year has added to my vision and enriched my life. Later when our teacher took the class into the nearby woods on a beautiful May day, when thousands of native pansies carpeted the forest floor, my eyes were opened to this exquisite beauty and from this first contact came growth with added knowledge and a greater appreciation of life. A new feeling, a new love for native soil or native land was developed, and a better understanding of life not of our making. Life became more joyful and more purposeful. Human intellect was raised to a higher plane by new thoughts, study, and appreciation. The voices of primitive soil can never be silenced—they may lie dormant but sooner or later they will break through the crust of stupidity, ignorance, and indifference to the eternal glory of our people and our common country.

LANDSCAPE APPRECIATION

Wisconsin Horticulture, May 1927

. . . When Burton Holmes in a recent lecture at Chicago was showing some beautiful views of the Grand Canyon, he said, "What wonderful compositions wouldn't Wagner have written if he had seen and felt the grandeur of this wonderful canyon." Whether we are Wagner or ordinary folks, the outstanding form of beauty and the most accessible to all and most cherished by the average man, woman and child, is the native landscape. Whatever race, whatever language we speak, our hills, our plains, our little brook and the sweet meadow that skirts it, the solitude of the woods, and the open sea, become a part of our life and will to a lesser or greater extent work their influence on us. Prof. Waugh says, "While painting and sculpture is available to comparatively few, while music does not appeal to everyone, while poetry is a taste of small party, the landscape is for all. Everyone loves the woods, the sea, the mountains, the sunset and the starry heavens."

Prof. Santyana in comparing the landscape with the products of the fine arts, like painting, sculpture, etc., says that the landscape has no form. This is misleading and incorrect. Take for instance the monadnocks on the prairies of Wisconsin, or Mt. Shasta with its beautiful snow covered top against the blue heavens, or any other subject—a tree, a flower—these forms are as definite as a painting or a piece of sculpture, and in the varied moods and colors of their surroundings may arouse a deep sense of appreciation and understanding. They have the power of reaching our finer feelings, those feelings that set the strings in motion, that produce the tender notes of poetry and music or any of the finer arts, and in this way pass on in a definite interpretation to other human beings. The landscape unadulterated by man is a finer thing than that which man calls his work. It has something of a spiritual nature that is beyond man's ability. There is a mystery and a charm about it that leads one into a new realm of untold beauty, full of inspiration and a freshness and vigor that stimulates you to action. It is a different world—a world not of our making, that opens visions of depth and grandeur, with endless themes and forms for study, for spiritual enjoyment, and for a richer and broader life. If the city gave all that is essential for a richer and higher life, there would be no pilgrimages to the country. . . .

As I now travel across the prairies in Illinois, rich in the purple of the woodlands along our streams, like etchings or woodprints, my memories go back to the purple hills of boyhood days, and life is relived once more. Does this not make for a richer life? It certainly reveals a world of beauty, seemingly free from struggles, from jealousy and hatred. It is a friendly world, something to love, something to tie to.

It is long ago now when one of my teachers took the class into a nearby woods—our first visit. The forest floor in certain sections was covered with thousands of native pansies, a carpet of exquisite beauty, and the first of its kind I had ever seen. From this first contact came growth with added knowledge and a greater appreciation of life. A new feeling, a new love for native soil and native land was developed, and a better understanding of the world not of our making. Life became more joyful, more purposeful. Human intellect was raised to a higher plane from new thoughts, study and appreciation.

To many, the prairie country is monotonous and uninteresting, but to us who have lived with it most of our lives it shows great breadth and freedom that works upon the imagination in many ways. There is a certain fascination and a drawing power in the purple ridges on the crest of a prairie wave that only those can understand who have watched them from boyhood up. Few who have been born and bred on the prairies are happy amongst the hills, with the vision shut in, and deprived of the beauty and the expanse of the far distant horizon. Its influence on the imagination and the character of the prairie man and woman is already evident, whether in arts, in poetry, in politics, or in masters of industry, and one can not foretell the growth of intellect due to the character molding by the prairie landscape. Masters like Louis Sullivan, Frank L. Wright, Walter Griffin, Vatchel Lindsay and Carl Sandburg are all of mid-America growth. It has inspired a distinct type of architecture, decorative design, and a new form of poetry, and some foreign artists say that there is more freshness and vigor in the work of our Mid-American novelist than found anywhere else in the western world. In politics and the industries we have such men as Lincoln and Henry Ford. Judging from present day happenings here will be the center of intellect and of power in these United States.

On a recent November day we were coming up over the hills back of Sturgeon Bay. Beyond to the north lay a broken landscape, its hill tops covered with birch and beech then in their soft greys and pinks, and all illuminated by the afterglow of the setting sun. We paused and thanked God that we had lived the day to see this great painting of the Master's Hand. Who doubts that such an impression is not of a higher order, and for the good and betterment of mankind? On a similar occasion some great American pointed out the beauty of the reflection of the sunset and said to me, "What a wonderful thing to be able to see this, and to appreciate it, and how much more we owe humanity that we have been given this vision." Is it not in this way that we take soundings with ourselves and see where we stand?

Those who have seen the rim of the oak forest, festooned with the delicate pink of the crab apple blossom, entwined in the silver and rosy buds of the oak, against the blue sky of May, must have been inspired by their color composition—a symphony of colors, so to speak. It is one of the many instances of nature's great ability in color composition and living picture making, something so fine that it leaves an impression on the human mind never to be forgotten, something that does truly inspire for the best and noblest in human life. Watch the flaky blossoms of the Juneberry in a snow storm, sweeping with the wind as if actually a part of the snow, revealing the struggles of life in the most romantic way; the tender blossoms in the blast of winter's day enjoying storm as it seems and surviving it as beautiful as ever. Let us call this a folk song.

Years ago we used to pilgrimage to a hill in southern Wisconsin covered with birch trees and a few Juneberries. There was a spiritual note in this grove of birches, and with the Juneberries in blossom, their delicate white entwined with the bark of the canoe birches, we could hear a spring sonata. You have heard McDowell's musical interpretation of the wild rose—one of the sweetest American compositions—but a wild rose was needed for its inspiration—and do you know that this great American composer left his wealth for the establishment of the Petersboro colony, when artists can study in God's Out-of-Doors.

We often are told of the thrill that the mountain flowers adjacent to the melting snow give to the visitor; but who has seen the delicate rosy blossoms of the trailing arbutus against a snow drift in early May in our own woods, and enjoyed its beauty, its daringness, and its joy over freedom won? Follow the trail on a beautiful spring morning and discover the first violet blossoms amongst the grasses. Shy and timid it hides from the world. There is no show, no pretense, no grandeur, but an exquisite beauty, so tender, so noble that it produces an immediate reaction on the mind. It demands a fine sense of color to feel and see its beauty. It makes you halt and think. The little friend has a daring spirit. It has to fight the battle of existence as courageously as the giant oak alongside of it. It gives so freely of its beauty and scatters its sweet perfume along your trail. I love its simplicity, its shyness, and its delicate beauty, and I wish that its message could touch the soul of every human being. Such a message makes life worthwhile. It stirs our imagination and awakens a love for friend and foe. It broadens our thought and lifts our minds out of bondage.

The grandeur of the towering mountains, cliffs, the moving dunes, the roaring sea, the babbling brook, and the silent river each and all have a message for us. There is the brilliant sunset or the poetic sunrise, the moonlit landscape and the starry heavens. These impressions are passed on to the subconscious mind, later to be expressed by the creative mind in many ways. The finest qualities of man can only grow in free air.

In primitive America are still visible the foot prints of the pioneer—the one that struggled with the wilderness, the one that hewed the trail for you and I, and the Indian and his life before him. Thus we are linked to the distant past, just like the old tree with its roots deep in native soil links us to past ages—a lesson in history for the imaginative mind. Birds sing to us and enliven the scenery with their beautiful plumage. Deer and partridge are denizens of the forest. Without them or any other wild life the silence of death hovers over the woodlands. There is a lesson of freedom and beauty in the act of the deer jumping across the trail that is not to be found in any Zoological garden, with its caged and confined animals. Destroy the wilderness and its spirit and you destroy yourself. Our country is swiftly filling up with human habitation, and the native landscape is encroached upon everywhere. The hum of machinery reaches every section of this earth, and the madness of modern life has a tendency to crush the finer feeling within us. At such times there is a strong urge towards the primitive for balancing up. It is here that the artist and the philosopher turn for new inspiration, for freshness, for vigor and strength of mind.

I have been trying to reveal to you the out-of-doors as it has penetrated my soul and influenced my life by a few inspiring pictures, (just a few words about which books might be written). It has taught me spiritual values that man has never been able to do. It has given me something to build my life's work on—a message pure and unadulterated, a message of beauty from the Master's mind. It is for you to partake of for the enrichment of your own life and for the enrichment of others. It speaks in many languages. It is a book beyond man's conception.

Watch the little moss, the first expression of life on the new made dune, or the lichen climbing up the barren face of a towering cliff—the beginning of things as it were. Only the truth is written here, and its message is of the finest kind. Listen to the voices of it all. It is the biggest thing on the earth, and the inspiration of every artist. To say it has no cultural value is not to know it, or not to know what life means.

THE NATURALISTIC TREATMENT IN A METROPOLITAN PARK

American Landscape Architect, January 1930

. . . Columbus Park, on the west side of Chicago, is as much an attempt to realize a complete interpretation of the native landscape of Illinois as anything which the author has done. Some of the work in close proximity to the refectory building was done after the author's authority had lapsed, and is not entirely in sympathy with the rest. Nature, however, has been kind, and, with the political management off its guard, many of the discrepancies have been covered with a profusion of growth.

The land originally acquired for this park consisted of prairie, with an abrupt slope on its eastern boundary, forming one of the ancient Chicago lake beaches. Most of the land had been subdivided and the parkways planted with trees, some of which still remain to tell the story. In the northeastern section, just above the ancient lake beach, stood the old farm buildings, practically on the same spot where the refectory building was built later. Generally speaking, the lands were flat like all the prairie lands west of Chicago, with the exception of the strip of beach. . . .

No park development worth speaking of has been done since the creation of Columbus Park, although a report on a Greater West Park system had been published by the West Chicago Park Commission at the time of the construction of Columbus Park. Some day the west side will find itself betrayed, and will feel the loss of park and playground which it needs for a healthful development of the hundreds of thousands of workers who have found their homes there. Columbus Park was at least an honest attempt to relieve a pressing situation which existed at that time. When, after two years of legislation, Harrison street was vacated by dedicating one hundred feet on the southern boundary of the park for street purposes, the opportunity for a bit of country within the city to which the people were entitled, became possible.

Now, for the beginning we had a prairie landscape, "checker-boarded" by trees that had been planted along the streets, an old beach with an elevation of from seven to eight feet, and a small nursery of soft maple trees planted by the sub-dividers in the northwest corner of the park.

The plan gradually took form in this manner. Below or following the ancient lake beach, a lagoon in the form of a prairie river suggested itself. To the east of the river there was sufficient land left for playgrounds, swimming pools, tennis courts, and utility buildings and yards. To the west and towards the sunset were the open prairies, near which stood the old farm building and a refectory building with a small garden. In the latter was a brook, the source of the prairie river. The surrounding broken landscape was suitable for outdoor plays or pageants, and council fire gatherings.

It was also proposed that the excavated material of the river should be used to form a ridge on the south border of the park so as to shut out the view of the adjoining railroads and factories. Jackson boulevard, which is a direct thoroughfare from the western limits of the city to Michigan boulevard, its eastern boundary, had to pass through the park. The problem was to fit it into the park landscape without destroying its purpose as a thoroughfare for fast-moving motor cars, and at the same time cut as little of the park as possible. This was accomplished by curving it gently towards the north. That part of the park, to the north of Jackson boulevard, left an abundance of space for a lovely lane of crabapples, plums and hawthorns. Each of the two corners of the northern section of the park provided ideal locations for tennis courts, readily accessible from the street, and so situated that they did not interfere with the general landscape of the park. . . .

The backgrounds of the swimming holes consist of rocky ledges of limestone, set in a natural way. This rock work forms a wall which gives seclusion to the bathers. It also introduces a bit of picturesque landscape with which most of the city children ordinarily would never come in contact. The author wanted them to feel and to know something of the beauty and poetry of the river canyons of this state. In the crevices of the rocks numerous rock plants have found their home.

There are two swimming holes—one from two to four feet deep, for bathers, and another from eight to nine feet deep, for swimmers. They are separated by what appears to be a fording place, so constructed that it is difficult to pass from the shallow pool to the deep. This is a safety measure, which makes it impossible to slide from the shallow to the deep water.

The recreation building, which adjoins, might have been more appropriate architecturally speaking. On the other side of this building is a small field for softball plays. This adjoins the children's playground. It contains a shelter with sand courts and a good-sized wading pool. In one corner of the playfield is a council ring. It is not what one would call a complete playground. Such a playground is found on the public school grounds only two blocks away. The former, however, has the real atmosphere of a park, with green lawns for the playfield and natural border planting. The wading pool has a rocky ledge towards the west, backed by a dense growth of plants. This makes for a fine setting and gives the children a lovely landscape picture. The plants used here may serve as a study of the flora growing in the immediate surroundings of Chicago. Numerous plants valuable to our birds have been planted on the border of the playground. Bird houses also have been provided so that the children may become acquainted with bird-life.

The council ring has been placed on an elevation about two feet above the playfield, at the edge of the woodland border. It is screened in and separated by several elm trees from the playground proper. The idea was to surround this spot with a little mystery, at the same time making visible the fire in the center of the ring, lighting up the forest border, and thus conveying to the children an impression of the campfires of the early pioneers. The ring in itself consists of a solid stone bench, about thirty feet in diameter, with a three-foot opening. The center of the ring has an elevation built out of the same rock about eight inches high and four feet in diameter on which the fire-wood is piled. A fire placed in this manner gives more heat; it also represents the open hearth. A few steps lead from the playfield to the council ring. Small playground apparatus is placed on a paved area near the shelter.

In the construction of the "river" the safeguarding of children who might accidentally fall into the water, and the erosion by wind action, were considered. A shelf was built about seven feet wide, running from a depth of one foot at the edge of the water to two feet at the edge of the shelf, then sloping at an angle of one to two feet to the depth of eight feet, the bottom of the lagoon. The shelves were then planted with native aquatic plants such as rushes, cat-tails, hibiscus, arrowheads and water lilies. This shoreline is ideal in more than one way, and has attracted the great blue heron into the heart of the city.

Reference has been made to the setting of the refectory building as a place for outdoor plays and council fires. The natural outdoor stage is separated from the audience by a brook. The space allotted to the audience, which is a lawn or a meadow, has a slope of about three feet. This slope is not perceptible in the landscape and yet it gives a little elevation for the spectators. The stage, or as it is called, the "Players' Hill," has two pits for natural fires by which the stage is lighted on dark nights. On moonlit nights no fire is required. Southwest of the stage, on a higher elevation, is a large council ring fifty feet in diameter which will take care of one hundred and fifty people or more.

The large meadow is used for a golf course, but in the construction of the green and the hazards, care was taken not to make them dominant or noticeable in the landscape. The first thing to be considered was a quiet pastoral scene. The southern part of the golf course forms a vale which is separated from the main field by appropriate planting. The river is visible at the eastern end of this vale and presents a peaceful scene that removes one far from the noisy city.

In general, the entire park landscape is a friendly one. Most of the trees used were of the type that will grow on low prairies. This excluded most of the hardwood trees, as the land was too heavy for their well-being. The planting, therefore, consisted largely of elm, linden, ash and cherry, with a few sugar maples and oaks in such situations as were favorable for them. The essential thing is to achieve a luxuriance of growth, and this can only be obtained where the land is suitable for the plants.

The border planting consists largely of crabapples, hawthorns, plums, sheepberries, ninebark, with a touch of gray dogwoods, choke cherry, red dogwoods in the lowlands, some hazel and prairie roses. For undergrowth among the trees gray dogwoods, witch-hazel, sheepberry, and viburnum are used. On the waterfront were added elderberry, bladder nut and yellow currant. Groups of crabapples and hawthorns extended out on the lawn, away from the border so as to break the monotony of a long border, a feature entirely native to our prairie landscape.

Prairie flowers, such as asters, goldenrod, coneflowers, phlox and shooting stars, were introduced in open places bordering the meadow; as undergrowth, Jacob's ladder, violets, spring beauties, trilliums, dogtooth violets and anemones were used. This undergrowth planting has never been finished, but it is the writer's hope that it will someday be completed.

The need of a true picture of our native landscape in parks and gardens of cultural value to our people, will grow with the growth of our cities. With the barrenness of road sites and the destruction of our primitive landscape will come a strong revival of interest in our own peculiar and fitting landscape beauty, and out of that revival will grow an art truly American. We have just begun to understand what landscaping can contribute to our culture, and we shall profit as a people by learning to understand more about it. We shall also profit by bringing to the many in our great cities a touch of such gifts Nature has bestowed for our enjoyment and which have made our home surroundings an inseparable part of our lives.

NATURAL PARKS AND GARDENS

The Saturday Evening Post, March 8, 1930

It will probably be news to most people who have driven over the extensive park system of Chicago that as late as 1885 little seventeen-acre Union Park that lies over on the West Side not far from the scene of the Haymarket Riot was the important park of the city. It had the zoological garden, and people came from far and near to see the bears and the eagles and the monkeys. Lincoln Park had just gone through its transformation from a cemetery to a park. Columbus Park was a waste land; Douglas, Garfield and Humboldt parks were only partly developed, as were the two big South Side parks, Jackson and Washington. That year, however, the animal house in Lincoln Park was finished and the animals were moved there, and after that Union Park was not such an attraction as it had been.

It was still in its heyday, though, when I applied for a job and was taken on as day laborer. I had had my technical training in Copenhagen and had spent three years sketching parks in Germany, but the day I came they needed a laborer and not a trained landscapist, and I needed money. In a year, however, I was foreman, and in 1894 I was made superintendent of Humboldt Park, and then consultant landscape architect. In 1920 I severed my connection with the west parks—or, more truly, politics severed it for me—and since that year I have been laying out private estates and parks in other cities. So much for biographical data. This is an article on gardens.

FORMAL BEDS AND FOREIGN PLANTS

Perhaps it might not be amiss to make just a brief statement of the history of the park system in Chicago. Chicago, for all its faults, is famous the world over for the vision of the men who have tried to give it beauty. First of these were those giants who in 1869 planned the present large park areas, with their continuous system of connecting boulevards. In no other city in the world can you ride for so many miles through parks and boulevards. Then there were those who planned the World's Fair; those who made the famous City Beautiful plan; those who in the beginning of the twentieth century established the playground system, and a few years later secured the enabling act for the forest preserves—that stretch of natural wooded and cut-over lands that lies like a great green belt around the city proper and its suburbs.

Lately the emphasis has been all on the lake front. I don't begrudge the beautifying of this, but I wish some group would undertake to establish numerous small parks through the congested West Side district. They need breathing spots there. To my notion, there should be a park area within walking distance of every city resident.

When, as foreman, I had my chance to design a garden, I laid out as formal a plantation as was ever made, and was quite proud of it. If any of the members of garden clubs or university landscape classes who have heard me lecture on natural gardens read this, they will probably smile. But at that time there was nothing else done. Every garden I had seen was formal. I still have some photographs of these early geometric designs in my office files, and occasionally a superintendent or draftsman will bring me one of them and inquire innocently, "Who laid this out, Mr. Jensen?" and I'll say, "Put it away. That's the folly of my youth." And I know that before it is put away there is a good deal of snickering at my expense. However, I can say for myself that I never did commit the crime of clipping trees into sculptural figures.

There were two reasons why I turned away from the formal design that employed foreign plants. The first reason was an increasing dissatisfaction with both the plants and the unyielding design—I suppose dissatisfaction with things as they are is always the fundamental cause of revolt—and the second was that I was more and more appreciative of the beauty and decorative quality of the native flora of this country.

NATIVE BEAUTY

In these formal beds the foreign plants didn't take kindly to our Chicago soil. They would die out no matter how carefully we tended them, and our propagating beds were kept busy growing replacements. And after a while I began to think, "There's something wrong here. We are trying to force plants to grow where they don't want to grow." And then I took less and less pleasure in looking at these formal designs. They were always the same. There was no swaying of leaves in the wind, no mysterious play of light and shade. And a garden should give more delight the more you look at it.

Then, too, as I said, I was becoming acquainted with the native trees and shrubs and flowers. One of the most vivid memories I have is my first view of a native crab-apple tree. It was on the train coming into Chicago, and through the car windows I saw silhouetted against the sky the delicate rose of a wild crab apple in early bloom. And when I was told it was a native tree, I said to myself, "That tree is a symbol of the beauty of this prairie landscape we have been passing through." And it still is to me today—it and the native hawthorn, whose gray horizontal branches are typical of the rolling lands of this mid-country. Nearly every Sunday and holiday, summer and winter, spring and fall, through those early years, I spent botanizing, studying and learning to know every plant that was native to this region. You see, in those days the city limits weren't so far out as they are now, and by riding to the end of a street-car line and then walking, one could see quite a number of plants in a day; and by taking the steam cars, one had a radius of thirty miles or so. And I was amazed at the richness of color in every season of the year, particularly in the fall. Northern Europe has some color in the autumn, but nothing to compare with this country. Some Japanese shrubs turn red— for instance, the barberry—but otherwise most of the important shrubs have a dull dead look that is decidedly uninteresting. And here were the lovely American shrubs that nature has adapted to the soil, completely neglected in park planting. Again I said something was wrong.

So I thought I would experiment by moving a number of these plants in and seeing how they looked and fared, and in 1888, in a corner of Union Park, I planted what I called the American Garden. As I remember, I had a great collection of perennial wild flowers. We couldn't get the stock from nurserymen, as there had never been any requests for it, and we went out into the woods with a team and wagon, and carted it in ourselves. Each plant was given room to grow as it wanted to. People enjoyed seeing the garden. They exclaimed excitedly when they saw flowers they recognized; they welcomed them as they would a friend from home. This was the first natural garden in Chicago, and as far as I know, the first natural garden in any large park in the country. To my delight the transplantings flourished and after a while I did away with the formal beds. There was now a period of expansion in the west park system, and the new areas, in Humboldt Park first, and then in Garfield and Douglas parks, were given over to me to design. A part of these parks had been laid out, and beautifully laid out, by Major Jenny, that picturesque figure whose name will go down in history as the designer of the first skyscraper. In the early days park design was done by gardeners, engineers or architects. The famous gardens of Versailles were laid out by Lenôtre, a gardener; the landscaping of our capital in Washington by the French engineer, L'Enfant; and when the west park system in Chicago was planned in the early 70's, the design was, as a matter of course, given over to a leading architect. Of late years the work has become specialized, and a number of universities now give training in land-scape architecture—Harvard was the first in this country.

The new areas gave me an opportunity of trying out on a large scale this idea of employing indigenous stock, and all the new shrubbery and trees that we planted were native and wherever replacements were needed in the older areas, these were largely made with indigenous material. Smoke is hard on green things, and parks that are situated in commercial and factory districts, such as Douglas and Garfield are, require a great deal of replanting, and consequently are expensive to maintain. It isn't only humans that suffer from breathing smoke.

A PIECE OF THE TROPICS IN CHICAGO

In these two parks there is quite a large area in lagoons—as much as we could have without interfering with the play space for the children; for in a congested district the children must have plenty of ground for recreation purposes. I believe that an inland park should have a great deal of waterscape. Water helps cool the air, it is beautiful to look at, and it provides facilities for boating, swimming, fishing and skating. In the flower garden in Garfield Park we installed a fountain device that made a mist of the spray, so that on sunny days a rainbow played continuously across the top of it. There would always be a crowd of people watching this. Then one dry summer the residents in the neighborhood had difficulty in getting the water to run from their third-floor faucets, and they complained that the fountain was using too much water. So the city ordered it turned off. I wanted the park board to install pumps that would permit us to use the same water over and over again, but they didn't see fit to make the appropriation, and the fountain has never played since, although the pipes are still there.

Speaking of Garfield Park brings to mind the Garfield Park conservatory. There had been small conservatories both in this park and in Douglas and Humboldt parks, and it required a lot of money to maintain and keep them in repair; also there was necessarily a great deal of duplication in the plant life they contained. I conceived the notion of putting all three conservatories under one roof, and since this was Chicago, and Chicago is accustomed to doing things on a big scale, I thought while we were about it, we might as well build the largest publicly owned conservatory under one roof in the world. The park board appropriated $275,000— I had wanted a larger sum for a larger building, but didn't get it—and in 1907 the conservatory was completed. Many persons called it Jensen's Folly; they predicted that glass wouldn't hold up in a building of such size, that a windstorm would smash it, that it couldn't be heated. But the conservatory is still there; it is still the largest in the world under one roof; last year more than half a million people visited it—there were more than 27,000 on one day—and the value of the plants in it was estimated in the annual report at nearly $1,000,000. And it is still one of the sights of Chicago.

Perhaps it might be interesting to tell an incident in connection with the designing of the palm and fern rooms, which face the main entrance. My idea in the first room was to show an idealized tropical landscape, and in the second room an idealized swamp scene. The first room was not so hard to arrange, but in the fern room we encountered difficulties. Since Chicago is in prairie country, I wanted this to have the feeling of the prairie, and we employed a stratified rock for the ferns to grow in. For the end of the room I designed a prairie rapids and a prairie waterfall. When the workman who was to build the waterfall had finished it, he expected me to praise him, but I shook my head. I said he was thinking of an abrupt mountain cascade, but here on the prairie we must have a fall that tinkled gently as it made its descent.

He tried again and again, but every day I said, "No, you haven't it yet."

Finally he said, "I can't do it any better."

I made no comment, but asked him if he could play Mendelssohn's Spring Song.

He looked at me in a startled way and answered, "No."

I asked, "Can your wife play it?"

"No."

"Do you know anyone who can play it for you?"

He thought a moment and then said they had a friend who was a good pianist.

"Well," I said, "you go to her house tonight and ask her to play the Spring Song over and over for you."

How to Build Waterfalls

This is what I heard later. He had gone home that evening, and the first thing he said to his wife was, "Jensen's gone cracked. He has so much work to do that it has at last affected his head." She asked what made him talk so, and he repeated the conversation. She considered a while, and then she said, "Maybe he meant something by it. Anyway, we'll go over to Minna tonight, and ask her to play." So they did, and the friend played the Spring Song for him four times. Then he jumped up, exclaiming, "Now I know what Jensen meant." And the next time I came, he stood to one side, smiling proudly. "Ah," I said, "you have heard the Spring Song." And the water tinkled gently from ledge to ledge, as it should in a prairie country.

Those who have been in the conservatory may remember the plain green slope of moss that lies between the brook and the waterfall. The contour of that slope was the most difficult small thing that I have ever done. I wanted it to give the feeling of greater depth to the room. It took me six months before I got it so that it satisfied me, but there isn't a line of it that has been changed since.

But this is indoor landscaping. Going back to the out-of-doors again, I want to tell you about the prairie river in Humboldt Park. As I made my Sunday excursions to the woods for the purpose of studying the native flora, I came to love the native landscape for its contours and physical aspects as well as for its plant life. It was God's out-of-doors—His own workmanship, as yet untouched by the hands of man. It seemed to me we all needed contact with this for our own spiritual development. Yet everyone from the city couldn't go to the out-of-doors, and the thought grew stronger and stronger with me that it was my obligation as a park man to bring this out-of-doors to the city. I do not mean by this that I was to try to copy Nature. A landscape architect, like a landscape painter, can't photograph; he must idealize the thing he sees. In other words, he must try to portray its soul.

So, in the new land in Humboldt Park, I designed the prairie river. It started in a little pool that seemed to well from some hidden source in the ground, then it trickled down as a brook in singing rapids over stratified rock, and then grew wider and wider until it made the stream that winds lazily, as a natural river does in prairie country. Along the edges we planted reeds and marsh plants, and the whole gave the feeling of a prairie landscape, and yet it is a city park. I put a prairie river in Columbus Park also when this was laid out in 1917. In fact, this whole park is a typical bit of native landscape idealized, as it appears near Chicago. The prairie bluff of stratified rock along the river has been symbolized with plant life. To the west extend the great lawns that symbolize the prairie meadow. These lawn areas are used for golf, but the greens are laid out in such fashion as not to destroy the horizontal aspect of the scene. Limestone rock from our native bluffs, with a backing of native forests, has been used in natural walls for the swimming pool and the wading pool for children.

IDEALIZING NATURE

This pool, when it was built, was the largest in any public park in the country—Chicago, again, you see, doing things on a big scale. The pool, or rather the swimming hole, was we have named it, is 450 feet long and will take care of 7000 a day. The deep pool has a depth of nine feet, and there is a wall between it and the shallow pool, so that the nonswimmers can't get into too deep water. The entrance to the pool is from the street. I always have a street entrance to every public swimming pool I have designed, for various reasons. For one thing, when boys come to a park to swim, they seem to have a single-minded notion that nothing else in the park matters, and they are apt to hit at branches of trees and to behave otherwise in a destructive way that they do not do when they come to a park for a walk or to play. And for another thing, it is disturbing to nonswimmers to have all these swimmers trooping past them. So everybody is made happy and at the same time the park is saved from thoughtless vandalism by this arrangement.

Columbus Park has special interest, too, because it is situated above and below one of the ancient Chicago beaches. The prairie river lies below the beach. The natural topography suggested such a layout.

Not only in parks but in private gardens as well, it has become my creed that a garden, to be a work of art, must have the soul of the native landscape in it. You cannot put a French garden or an English garden or a German or an Italian garden in America and have it express America any more than you can put an American garden in Europe and have it express France or England or Germany or Italy. Nor can you transpose a Florida or Iowa garden to California and have it feel true, or a New England garden to Illinois, or an Illinois garden to Maine. Each type of landscape must have its individual expression.

But in trying to make a garden natural, we must not make the mistake of copying Nature, as I said before. Copying Nature is only one step removed from copying another garden. Art idealizes; it is creative, and a reproduction is only a reproduction, no matter how fine and noble the model is. The landscape garden must have a dominant thought or feeling in it, just as a great painting must have a dominant thought in it. To me, that feeling should be spiritual; it should be love for the great out-of-doors, for the world that God made. Such a garden will be a shrine to which one may come for rest from the strife and noise of the man-built city. It will have in it the mystery of the forest, the joy and peace of a sunlit meadow, the music of a laughing brook, the perfume of flowers, the songs of birds, the symphony of color in tree and shrub.

A Spot of Sunlight

And the elements one works with are the contours of the earth, the vegetation that covers it, the changing seasons, the rays of the setting sun and the afterglow, and the light of the moon.

When I plan a garden, I do not make a single pencil mark on paper until I have the complete picture of the whole composition in my mind. And the composition is never a matter of many things, but of a few things that will blend harmoniously every season of the year, and that will also suit the temperament of the client.

Sometimes I start with the setting of the house. If the home is not already built, I choose the location and, together with the house architect, decide on the material out of which the house is to be built, and on the color, so that it will blend into the surrounding landscape. Always the house should have a setting of trees. I am fond of quoting the Norwegian poet Björnstjerne Björnson's lovely poem, "Hidden by trees you find my home." The home should be a retreat away from the public eye. Sometimes I start with the road that curves away from the public highway to the house. I say "curves," for in the composition of an important road I never use a straight line— Nature's lines are curves, and I believe, with the ancient Greeks, that the curve is the line of beauty. But the road should never be serpentine; there should always be a reason for the curve, and the road should always be in shadow, emerging upon the lawn in full sunlight. Sometimes I start with the open meadow as my keynote. I always have a clearing in every garden I design—a clearing that lets in the smiling and healing rays of the sun. A sunlit clearing invites hope. George Inness, whom I consider the greatest landscape painter this country has produced, always has a ray of light in every picture he painted. No matter how storm-tossed the clouds are, there is this ray of hope promising a better day. I am never in the Art Institute of Chicago without making a visit, if only for a few minutes, to the splendid Inness collection there. And every time I come away refreshed. Inness was a great master.

Perhaps I will make this matter of design more clear if I give specific examples of what various problems have been and how they have been solved.

One of the first private estates I laid out was for a big corporation attorney who was of a very nervous temperament. He had been offered a number of places and he gave me the responsibility of making the choice. I selected the site that had a meadow over which the sun set both winter and summer; for, with his office in the city, my client could be home to enjoy his garden only during the late afternoon and evening. Toward the south was a low depression where water stood most of the year. It was in the line of the moon, so I placed an informal pool at that point, and backed it with red cedars in order to get the reflection of the moon and the dark mystery of the cedars' shadows in the water.

To the east was Lake Michigan; part of the open exposure here was planted out to keep the cool winds away from the porch during the early morning and evening. At one corner we planted sugar maples and sumac. Here the afterglow of the setting sun in autumn would illuminate their gay plumage, and against the purple background of water and dusky eastern heavens would give a note not unlike that of Wagner's *Tannhäuser*.

The kitchen garden was planted to the north, and, as the space was small, we built a wall to protect the cut flowers and vegetables from the north winds. Where more space is available, I use hedges for protection to the kitchen garden. This is the only spot in a garden plan where I think hedges are allowable.

Several years after the garden was finished, I was invited to dinner by the owner, and, as we sat smoking on the porch, with the full moon playing on the pool and the dark cedars making black shadows, he said to me, "When I've had a hard day downtown, there are only two things that can rest me—the sunlight on the meadow when I come home, and then, later, the pool of water." So you see this garden had suited the temperament of the client.

On another estate the house was built facing a depression that was too wet for trees, with the east front on Lake Michigan. Part of this depression ran into a forest of oaks on the west side of the estate. The whole depression was cleared of its small shrubs and made into a lawn. The thought back of this was that through this long opening during the fall the setting sun could be seen from the house enlivening the oaks in their autumn red, thereby giving the whole landscape a more brilliant color than would otherwise be possible. We named this the Path of the Setting Sun. Another interesting problem on this estate was the fact that the entrance gate was on ground that was higher than the site of the house.

Now, the house, to be commanding, should seem to be the higher. You want to go up to a house, not down to it. This is how we solved that difficulty. To the left was a bit of natural woodland, which we augmented with some planting, and a little farther on was a ravine. The road was made to go through this woodland and planting, and then to skirt the ravine, and so, when the house emerged quite suddenly to view over the lawn, you had no thought of its being lower. It seemed higher, and yet the road was not long.

REVEALING THE HOUSE

On the Edsel Ford place near Detroit, we had the problem of making the house seem higher than the road in an absolutely level country. Lake St. Clair, a rather shallow lake, lies to the west of the house. By making the road follow the margin of this lake and planting out the view of the house until the right point was reached, and then letting the house emerge suddenly, it was possible to give the effect of a greater rise than the few feet there actually are.

An entirely different situation was offered at Mr. Ford's summer home on the coast of Maine. Here is a mountainous country consisting largely of granite rocks. There was no difficulty in getting a commanding site for the house; the problem was to anchor earth for plants to grow in. So we had to confine ourselves to a small garden, and this was accomplished by building walls and filling in so as to secure a level surface. The garden was constructed out of native rocks and plants, with native evergreens for a background, and with an informal pool under a bit of cliff. In place of grass, we used carpets of dwarf mountain plants. The entrance to the garden was treated in a similar fashion, and as the home is built out of the same stone as the garden, quarried right on the grounds, the whole represents an expression of what can be done with the material at hand of that region. I have had as much pleasure in making this garden as I have had in any garden I have designed.

Down in the blue-grass region of Kentucky, where limestone is everywhere, I was asked to remodel an estate that had been landscaped some years before in the formal manner. Not far from the house was a natural sink hole, so common in Kentucky, and it was the formal garden that had been laid out in the bottom of this that was the particular eyesore of the owner. My thought was that this sink hole would make a lovely rock garden, with rocks set on the edge of the bowl and interspersed with cedars, flowering dogwood and other characteristic trees of the region. So it was developed. There was a pool with water lilies that reflected also the plants growing above it, and then there were shady nooks for ferns and sunny ledges for sun-loving rock plants. This garden was entered from a lane that connected up with a vegetable garden and orchard. I had not visited this garden for many years until a year ago last spring, and then I found it full of mystery, and the owner said it was a retreat he liked to go to. This, you see, was a bit of old Kentucky idealized.

GARDENS FOR SMALL HOMES

On a hillside place in Tennessee, facing the Smokies, the problem was to see both the beauty of the valley below and to bring the mountains, so to speak, to the door. In other words, to arrange the contours of the land near the house in such a way that you felt the mountains coming to you. This was done by making the slope from the porch concave, so that the eye could follow the whole slope down into the valley. Toward the right the concave line was terminated abruptly by coming forward with the slope and planting it with trees native to the hillside, thus producing the effect of rolling lands beyond, while the forest-covered hill close by seemed united with the planted trees. A little path edged with ferns led through the grove and helped give the feeling of going into a forest. The effect of this whole arrangement was that the character of the surrounding territory seemed to terminate right at the door.

At the home of Mr. Julius Rosenwald on the north shore of Chicago there were numerous difficulties on account of the narrow width of land, between Lake Michigan and a ravine running almost parallel to it, on which the house was built. A spur of a smaller ravine, however, entered the large ravine almost opposite the house to the west. This made possible a lawn that extended itself into this small ravine, revealing the high land on the opposite side in a way that made it look like a high hill. Incidentally this view was in the path of the setting sun. Hawthorns, crab apples and prairie roses planted along the edge of the ravine prevented anyone being conscious of a deep ravine directly on the edge of the lawn, and also gave color and light to the meadow in the spring. The setting sun illuminates this planting, too, in a most charming way in the fall. The ravines were utilized by putting in tanbark trails and by planting native flowers on the slopes, so that these became beautiful gardens. The main entrance drive was made to come down another spur of the ravine, and is entirely unseen from the residence or the lawn. The idea of this estate is to give the feeling of a country made beautiful by deep ravines.

At the south of the house is a pool for the reflection of the moon, with a background of native woodlands, whose floor is covered with wild flowers. I have used wild flowers on an extensive scale in other places also. For instance, on a hill slope of an estate in Freeport, Illinois, we planted thousands and thousands of black-eyed Susan and goldenrod, and you can imagine how refreshingly yellow this slope was through the summer and early fall. And on another estate we planted the purple coneflower. The flat-topped purple seed pod of this stays on during the winter, too, and when the snow is on the ground the pods reflect a lavender tint on its surface— a very lovely effect. Aside from its beauty, a field of wild flowers is practical, too, for it obviates a great deal of lawn cutting.

Just one other example—a small estate of scarcely an acre. But this was large enough to have woods so dense that they hid the street. And there are two sun openings, one at the front of the house, and the other spreads out from a sun room that connects the house and garage. In the latter we put a bird pool, because the owners are great bird lovers, and whatever shrubs and plants we brought into this place are the kind the birds like. A little lane, planted with violets, led to a council ring, with a fire in the center, in the southwest corner of the property. Around the council ring were planted Western crab apples and violets, so, you see, in the spring there is a rose bloom overhead and a blue carpet underneath. To the north was a grove of native crab apples and hawthorn that we left untouched, except for a path leading through them from the council ring to the kitchen garden. This garden contains apple trees, black-berries, gooseberries, currants and grapes, besides beds for vegetables and cut flowers nearest the house, and it has much sunlight. Economically, the garden is a success, and viewing it from the house, it has an air of domesticity that is essential.

As a minor note, I often bring into my compositions a council ring, which consists of a ring built of stone, of a diameter of nineteen to twenty feet, and with a fireplace in the center, with an elevation of eight to ten inches above ground. The idea of the ring is partly Indian and partly old Nordic, though the construction is modern. Practically the ring brings people close together, and the fire chases away the mosquitoes, so often an annoying hindrance to our enjoyment of the out-of-doors. From a spiritual standpoint, there is something within us that loves the fire, and gathering about it has a social leveling effect that puts us all on a par with one another. A council-fire gathering is the most democratic institution-we have. We are, after all, children of the primitive, and we like to go back to it.

Very often I make a combination of outdoor swimming pool and stage. I always elevate the stage, and I call it "players' hill," for I believe the stage should be looked up to rather than depressed as the Greek stage was. The swimming pool usually has a background of rock—here on the plains, of lime or sandstone, for besides being native, their horizontal strata typify the prairies—and in granite country, granite. On top of the elevation is the actual stage, backed by cedars or groups of deciduous planting, depending on the environs and the composition of the rest of the landscape. The stage is lighted by natural fires from one or two depressed fire pits. This natural firelight gives a wavering, mysterious appearance to the faces of the actors that no artificial lighting can do, and the movements of the actors are reflected in the pool below in a most poetic way. The pool serves also to separate the audience from the players, and as a carrier for the voices. Where there is no pool, I make a players' hill by slightly elevating a corner of the garden. The players' hill should always face the moon, so that on moonlight nights plays can be produced with no other lighting. Perhaps it might interest you that in the latest pool we built we also incorporated a sun bath; keeping up with the times, you see.

No Fences or Hedges

The large estates, of course, are only for a few people. I am asked every once in a while, as other landscape architects are asked, what suggestions I would make for the designing of a small garden that must be laid out and tended by the owner himself. Naturally, I believe that this, like the public park or the large private estate, should be planted with the trees and shrubs and flowers that are native to the surrounding landscape, with the addition, of course, of old-fashioned garden flowers and shrubs, such as the lilac, hollyhock, oleander, geraniums—plants that the white man has carried with him wherever he has gone and that have become through the centuries household pets, just as the dog and the cat are. In a desert section, there should be desert plants, in a mountainous section, mountain plants, and in a prairies section, prairie shrubs and flowers. Then one will at least be certain that, given a little care, the garden will grow.

To my mind, the ideal location for the small house on a small lot is about forty feet back from the walk. There should be a lawn in front with a few trees, and if the ordinances of the town permit, some shrubbery should be planted in the parkway. This gives the feeling of privacy to the entrance. There should never be any shrubbery planted against the walls of the house, unless there is some uninteresting space that had best be covered. The architecture of the house should be allowed to reveal its full beauty, and this it cannot do if it seems sunk in a mass of shrubbery, as if it were in a swamp. If the house is covered with vines, then the source of the vine should show— it has its own beauty.

Fences destroy the peacefulness of the scene. If used, they are least objection-able if not more than three feet high. And no clipped hedges! Hedges are useful only when they serve as a windbreak, and a windbreak is not needed next to the street. However, I am not much concerned that the clipped hedge will become a permanent feature of the American town scene. Clipped hedges require a great deal of work, and the American home owner is too fond of golfing and motoring to put in many hours with the clipping shears.

The flower garden should be in the back, and the vegetable beds can be sepa-rated from the rest of the garden by beds of flowers that are frankly meant for cutting. Flowers for cutting should be planted in rows the same way that carrots are. The or-namental flowers can be planted along the paths or spaces against the house, but they shouldn't be crowded or packed like sardines. Compression is against the rules of art. A plant should be given all the room it needs, and then its individual beauty will stand out and we grow to love it for itself, and our enjoyment of the garden is greatly enhanced. A garden without love has no story. There should be a festival of color in the flowers that bloom in the spring, and a glory of color in the foliage of the plants that are at their best in the fall of the year. And there should be some flowers for perfume in a garden. Trees can be associated rather closely together, but not any closer than will permit the ground floor to grow plants that like the shade. If possible, the garage should be hidden with planting.

There should be few paths, and they should not be of cement or brick. For a formal path raked gravel is best. Paths of stone with grass in between are much softer to the eye. But stone in a garden must always be used with care. Too much stone is cold and makes a garden lose its friendliness.

Sometimes it is interesting to introduce a rock garden, because then one may have plants that cannot express their full beauty otherwise. Rock plants become flat in a border, but crawling over rocks for sun, their struggle is a picture worth having. Associated with the rock garden may be a pool where the birds may drink, and where fish may make one contemplate their manner of life. The pool should be in the background, so it can have a setting of shrubs, whose shadows will bring the mystery of the forest and at the same time give it shade to the plants that want it.

But above all, a garden should be individual. It should not be like one's neighbor's, for then it is monotonous; it should express the personality of the owner. If one likes birds, one should plants shrubs the birds like; if one likes Shasta daisies, they should be the prominent feature. But a garden that is fitted for a hillside should not be put on a plain, or vice versa.

It is not size that makes a garden beautiful. It is the love that you give it and the spirit of the out-of-doors—of God's out-of-doors—that is in it.

CONSERVATION IN THE REGIONAL PLAN

Conference on State & Regional Planning Keynote, April 26, 1934

We are living in an age in which it seems to me we take too much for granted. Pass a resolution—and it becomes law? We see and accept too much theory and too little practice, and yet the practical mind is the one that gets to the top of the ladder. Creative ability is so rare that one needs a microscope to find it—and yet here is the source and the fountain for creative work in abundance all about us only to be ruthlessly destroyed because man has become blinded by the false lights of a so-called civilization.

It seems to me that, in spite of many good resolutions and high-sounding words, we are still far from the goal of true conservation. Many well-meaning folks want conservation if it can be had with some personal gain. You can't compromise on conservation of the primitive with its mute life. It is either complete conservation or it is not.

Nature resents a disturbance of its balance and we suffer the consequences. The city mind—the mind from the asphalt and concrete pavement—exerts too great an influence upon the rural country. Its path of destruction can be seen radiating out into God's out-of-doors from all our large cities. Someone has said that the wilderness must be subdued for the millions. It is rather the millions that must learn the language of the wilderness or there shall be no wilderness and no culture of worth.

Some day the rural mind—the mind close to the soil—will rise in its full force and exterminate the "weeds in our city culture," and the result will be beauty every-where. The habit, and a bad one it is, to burn over hedgerows, woodland, and field in early spring must have had its origin in the country, but at a time when such burning was a clearing process to get bread and butter. Today this habit has become one of the greatest outrages to a beautiful country. It seems so absurd to think that this method will destroy all the bad things of the open country, when the result is death to beauty and health to weeds of all kinds. I have seen fires started purposely when our song-birds were on their nests. What has become of Christian love?

Our native game fairs no better. The many game refuges are only so in name. Every time the papers herald a new game refuge the hunters increase by the thousands in our large cities. And how absurd to take the hunters' money to pay the expense of such refuges, including raising game-birds, at the expense of final extermination of our native birds in our State parks and in place of protecting the game in these parks, show the visitors caged animals: The city boy and girl should see them free and have the thrill of seeing them jumping across the trail as a profound education to them. They can see caged animals a plenty at home.

What we need is education in conservation of our wild animal and plant life—departments in conservation in our schools and colleges. Let the hunters' money go to such education and not to increase the hunters by preserving more game for them to kill that may lead to complete annihilation of our native wild life. Keep the balance of nature unmolested or we shall reap the consequences.

It should become a habit to talk about conservation like, for instance, baseball—to talk about the beauty of our native land—our home—our fireside, and to know and understand the real meaning of this. We should be proud of lovely roadsides, our woodlands, clean lake shores, undefiled streams, lovely farmsteads under the shade of noble trees surrounded by the sweet perfume of apple blossoms, and all the beauty, the peace, and loveliness that God's out-of-doors has to offer us.

Think less about planning and more about the freedom of doing things with a full understanding of its real purpose and its lasting good for all. Don't put the rural country into a straight-jacket! Conservation of God's beautiful creation is a real job. It has its roots deep into native consciousness—sings of by-gone days, and fills your Soul with hope for the tomorrow. It can only be accomplished by everybody helping and doing his best for real accomplishment—by doing his bit and doing it well for the betterment and for the good life of all.

A PROGRAM FOR SCHOOL
OF THE SOIL

Undated Typescript, mid-1930s

Environments exert great influence on humans, both for the good and the bad; the imagination of the boy or girl is enlarged and inspired by contact with the out-of-doors, and the message from the primitive is fundamental in human progress, whatever that may be.

Freedom must be absolute, but not without responsibilities, otherwise freedom may become a license. The golden rule is the only rule for any kind of education. To be yourself, to respect the rights of others, to do your part well for the joy of doing it must be fundamental for this school or any other school of the fine arts.

Grades, examinations, promotions, degrees or medals, or any other method that has the tendency of marking out the individual, are not conducive to good character building. Each student must feel the joy and the full reward in his own accomplishments for work well done. This is Democracy—spiritual Aristocracy. I believe that any student of this, or of any school of the arts, must be aristocrat in that sense, and that they should be sent out as interpreters of a new order in the art of living. Almost all advance made by the human race thus far has been done by small minorities.

There should be no set rules. Students visiting such a school as this, must have within them a reasoning power of a higher order, that taboos man-make rules and regulations, which only in the long run tends to retard freedom—God made man free. It is easier and more convenient to follow authority than to think for himself.

Arts cannot be classified. There is no superiority, no inferiority. We are all equal in the higher sense of life. I believe that Landscaping is equal in importance to any of the arts as a medium of expressing what is fine and noble in art. The building of parks, and the restoration of man-scarred earth, is great in their contribution to cultural life. The square and compass must be counteracted by the message of the out-of-doors, or there can be no escape from learning degenerating itself.

Learning, in a broader sense, should be based on the spoken word and the family group. In other words, there should be no books of instruction. The students will have to make notes of what they hear if they cannot remember it.

In that way they are free to select what they want or what interests them most. It is the living word that is the great intercourse between mankind much more so than the written word, and whether this living work is spoken by the master of the art of whether by the student in the debates, it has a lasting power. The living work goes deeper into human consciousness under the starry heavens, or in the deep silence of valley or forest. To exclude this from this school is to omit the spark that kindles the fire of creative ability.

All students attending this school would have to belong to the family group. By that is meant that every student would have to live in the dormitories and partake in the evening life. The group idea is the idea of home life, out of which will grow a lasting friendship so essential in our daily lives.

The studies should be divided into professional and cultural. The amount of students must necessarily be small and less than twenty-five. Mob psychology is not conducive to a higher development of the human kinds.

A major part of the studies should be in the out of doors, interpreting the landscape in its various moods—the growth and fitness of individual and group plants in relation to topography, and the influence of changing lights and shadows. In other words, when the out of doors is in a particular mood the landscape should be interpreted to the students at that moment. The out of doors is not a stationary thing like an artificial stage. Its changing ways exert its invaluable influence on the landscape for all of us. Excursions to the various types of landscape of the region are essential for a better understanding.

The Professional studies would include the study of Ecology, Topography, Soil Studies. Ecology would include the study of the native flora. The native fauna must also be a part of the studies. The cultural studies would include Painting, Poetry, Drama, Music, Architecture, Literature. Each student is required to give a part of each day for the cultivation of fruits and vegetables needed for consumption.

The evenings should be used for discussion and debate on matters that are of human value. Some of the evenings ought to be open to the public, perhaps more in the way of lecturing than debating. All study hours and all evening debates must begin and end with singing.

Entrance examinations are essential to find out the student's special fitness for the subject he wants to study. In other words, no one should be permitted to the school that did not possess a deep feeling for the art, not for the sake of making money but studying it for the love of the art and for the service he might give to his fellow man. The material reward will not fail him. If later, students are found lacking in interest or fitness they will be asked to leave. The students may leave the school at the end of any month. There will be no set time for the course of studies. A certificate for the period in attendance will be given the student upon leaving the school. The students must keep their own room clean and supply their own laundry. Each room should be occupied by three or four students.

The teaching force should consist of two or three permanent teachers, one of them the authoritative head. Most of the teaching should be done by visiting teachers that are masters in the arts. They would have more bearing on the life of the student than just an ordinary teacher who for a small sum of money has been hired to teach. Many of these visiting teachers may be willing to give their lectures gratuitously being furnished with food and lodging and having the privilege of taking their family with them. Permanent teachers should be drawn from the student group and replaced with new blood from time to time.

The native landscape must be the source and foundation for all studies. There must be created in the minds of the students a love and appreciation for the things that are and always will be home. Visiting teachers are to bring in their ideas from the world beyond—a flow of thoughts that will enrich the mind of the student and give a clear knowledge of the work and thoughts of other peoples. The school should work out its own problems from time to time, and there should be no set program to start with. A poet should lead—to great accomplishments or failure— but lead singing.

For the school proper there should be à hall for lectures, a large dining room, a kitchen and servants quarters, dormitories for the students and quarters for the teachers. These should all be of the simple kind, fitting to the woods of which they are a part. Extravagance in school buildings and equipment are detrimental to a wholesome growth. We have shown entirely too much extravagance not only in school buildings but in dormitories, fraternity houses, etc., much of which the student never can acquire during his life time, consequently leading him into false standards of living. It is out of the simple things that great things grow. For out of door discussions and studies a council ring should be provided, and for dramatic art there should be a player's hill.

There will also be a summer school for all the arts during July and August. This summer school will be separate from the regular school. The students from the regular school would have the privilege of attending the summer school.

Students must be limited to 25, divided into small groups. Each group should have its own council ring. For lectures or large gatherings the council ring of the school should be used. The beauty and the real value of the primitive is destroyed as soon as great congregations enter into it. The evenings should be given up to discussion and debates around the council fire. The spoken work should rule supreme. There should be excursions to the various types of landscapes found in the region, each with its own message and its own beauty.

The students will be housed in tents but the hall as well as the dining room and other accommodations could be used by the summer students during the period that the regular school is closed. Here, as well as in the regular school students would have to do their own cleaning and tend to their own laundry. Three or four students should occupy one tent.

The public should not have daily access to the camp or the school grounds. Visiting days so announced are necessary to prevent any interference with the out of doors studies. There might well be arranged a lecture program for visiting days.

In connection with the school of the soil, it might be of great value to the students to establish an art colony within walking distance for the sake of intercourse between the regular students and the painters and sculptures, or any other artists that may desire to live here for the summer months. I have always thought that such an intercourse is of tremendous value to the student of any profession as a great deal of his work today is more of the professional rather than of an art nature. The consequence is, too many professional men have no thought nor any real feeling for the art—a most unfortunate situation if the arts are to live. To get the art mind is one of the very essential things for the professional man of today and an intercourse with artists is very helpful. The country in which the school is to be located being beautiful and acceptable for artists to live in, there should be no trouble in creating such a colony.

Copied from an undated typescript from the mid-1930s, attributed to Jens Jensen

THE "CLEARING"

Die Gartenkunst, September 1937

. . . [My] house was built by the first residents, who came to this area as farmers, about 100 years ago. It is the characteristic blockhouse of those pioneers, who beat/fashioned out of the ancient forests the nutritional foundation for our grand cityscapes.

My living room was for a long time the first and only school room in the settlement. I had the originally flat roof changed; it was raised, both for practical and for aesthetic reasons. Steep roofs last longer; the rain runs off faster; the snow doesn't stick as much. More important than these considerations, it seemed to me, was the expression of true Germanic architecture, which, for me, is unthinkable without the steep roof. The flat roof, on the other hand, is an element of the romantic and oriental architectures.

The Spirit of America, wanted or unwanted, is in and around my house. The rooms are kept in colors long since common/usual in this country, [colors] which clearly go back to influences from the Indians. Countries and landscapes often have—as they have certain forms—also color compositions which, ever returning, become a recognizable signal. One might think just for example of the rural areas in Pennsylvania, not yet spoiled by industry and city life, which are ruled over sovereignly by a style of wooden architecture which is uniformly painted with oxen blood, whereby, in a strange color contrast, blue window shutters hang on the gloomy-red walls of the house. The American original inhabitant is color-happy; he is excited by certain color combinations, which have found their way into creations of the White Man.

The sensibilities of the American for the fantastical symphonies of color in modern neon advertising might be connected unconsciously with the colorfulness with which the Redskins decorated their household implements, their clothing, yes, even their bodies in times of war. And so the walls of my living room have maintained, without my even thinking about it, a colorful frieze, and a whole series of household items [have maintained] a similar paint job. This is strange, and I often I'm amazed by it; still, such doings are harmless. . . .

A singularity of my living room might perhaps interest the reader: the ceiling of the same is the roof of the house. In this way it was possible to install an especially high window on both ends of the room. Such openings allow a comfortable and un-imagined enjoyment of the outdoors. One sees up into the tops of the very closest trees; one sees half of the starry skies; sees the sun and the moon come and go down.

But now to the surroundings of the house. . . . It goes without saying that I only had as many trees felled as was necessary for proper sunning of the house and a pleasant garden area. Also some visual paths were cut through to beautiful points in the landscape, especial to a nearby body of water. An opening to the north was added in order to be able to view the light from Northern Lights on cold winter days. Some Betula papyrifera died after this clearing work, proof that they were not in agreement with my intervention.

The complementing plantings which I then undertook are simple and basically indigenous. I am a great friend of the indigenous treasure of plantlife and hate it when nurseries indiscriminately pour their specimen collections into our gardens. A group of Prunus americana provide a special joy to my home when they stand in their snow-white Spring flourish. The Malus coronaria, an indigenous wild apple, Viburnum prunifolium, as well as groups of indigenous wild roses—Rosa blanda, Rosa setigera, Rosa humilis, and Rosa carolina—play large roles. At the entrance to the piece of land stately groups of lilacs survive that appear to be ancient and are sure to stem from the first settlers. Especially the lilac pushed along with the block house of the Europeans westward and is today one of the most beloved bushes in the New World. Quite often the observant hiker finds in clearings within the deepest woods or on the widest barren grasslands of our country troops of the most wonderful lilacs. Even if the very last traces of human activity have disappeared from around the same [lilacs], certainly once a house stood here, the homestead of someone of our courageous, undaunted predecessors. Be it that its dwellers fell at the battle ax of the Indians, that the drought burned the seeds, or merely that better fields coaxed them further westward; for some reason they left the area, and only the lilacs remind us of them.

Basically, indigenous wood types should dictate the work of the garden and landscape designer, but there is also nothing to object to when species are used by the house which remind us of our Nordic homeland on the other side of the great body of water. Thus I am a great friend of the Scottish fence rose Rosa rubiginosa, and its powerful defenses remind me again and again of the bloody gashes on arms and legs [gashes] which I in my younger years reaped in wild play. Then there are also a bunch of climbing mallow and phlox, a gift of a German immigrant who has long gone to the Happy Hunting Grounds. In addition there were all kinds of lilies and some indigenous shrubs which were effortlessly settled in the vicinity of the house and which entirely give the impression of being coincidental. In the vicinity of the kitchen lies the small, purposefully laid out flower and herb garden, the wards of which are earmarked only for use in the house. Somewhat more distant, in the line of sight toward the body of water, broad areas of high wild shrubs spread themselves out, [shrubs] which integrate themselves harmonically with their woodsy surroundings. . . .

Of all these plants Solidago is one of my favorites. There is, however, hardly anything more impressive than the stately Goldenrod, which rules our indigenous forest clearings in giant numbers. Even the tuft of dried out seed remnants on its long stem lends the desolation of the wintry vegetation scene a special charm. Dim witted "garden friends" cut these off and in that way "protect" the root system: what a loss of beauty and charm!

And thus there is nothing in my home and garden that could somehow disturb the peace and noble simplicity of the wild nature. Even though some "foreigners" like the lilac, the Scottish fence rose, and the climbing mallow have found a foster home here, their appearance in the vicinity of the house doesn't have any disturbing effect.

In summary, I must admit: I love this spot of earth more than everything [else] which I ever created. I love it because of its familiar beauty, sprung up out of the landscape, its panoramic views, its ancient stone formations, its 1000 year old junipers, its smiling birches, and most especially because of its colorful oaks, maples, and beeches that are able to give us that Fall bonanza of colors which no other continent can surpass.

Translation from the German "Die 'Lichtung,'" by Margarete R. Harvey, ASLA

GARDEN DESIGN:
SPECIAL LECTURE

Internationaler Gartenbau Kongress, Berlin, 1938, 1939

Human footprints scatter themselves all over this earth. They are found through the valleys, over the mountains, across the moors, the desert, the cultivated fields, or wherever human habitation has resolved itself into communities. They are visible in great boulevards, in simple highways, in by-ways and footpaths. The further one is removed from the density of population, the more intimate, the more inspiring, the more instructive in the world not of our making, these trails become.

It is along such a trail, where the footprints of the Indians before us are still visible, that I often wander. Here is peace and quiet. One can think deeply and profoundly without interruption from Man's inventive genius, which is not always enjoyable and understandable. Such trails as this one have always given me much to think about. The feeling of the past while looking into the future, is not surpassed anywhere else in this world of ours. There are the traditions of the footprints before and there is the growth of the trail as time goes on. It is a thing in its making.

The small bayous; the sun openings surrounded by deep shadows of ancient trees with their roots deep in native land; the far distant views, the vision which calls one beyond ones own shores far into the distance and with it the thoughts of the future far away on the horizon that the vivid imagination catches a glimpse of; the intimate beauty of friendly flowers which greet you and brush your feet as you pass them by; a rock covered with mosses and lichens, another world so to speak; century old trees now lie on the forest floor, resting softly in deep mold, covered with a forest of tiny plants expressing a new world, a world in its making, giving sustenance and nourishment to the grandeur that will be the tomorrow, are all impressions that was never found within the walls of any room, anywhere.

This trail is rather adventurous. It challenges you to conquest. Now it lies four feet under a white blanket of snow, and to the west, and the northwest, and the north east are ice fields as far as the eye can reach, and over these ice fields the storm sweeps down from the cold northwest, from the great arctic of everlasting ice and snow. It sings a peculiar song and fills one with vigor and strength and determination.

The trail follows rugged cliffs, skirting turbulent waters, and on these cliffs hang, so to speak, tiny flowers that one would little expect in these whereabouts, daring the tempest and enduring the arctic colds of winter. Here thousand year old trees, that in their endeavor to live, crush the rocks and make food for themself.

The Park and Garden Planner finds hundreds of motives for parks and gardens along this trail; motives for gardens of a few feet, a tiny nook with its inspiring beauty, its soft rays of sunlight in the depths of the mysterious woodlands; motives for large gardens; and motives for parks of tens of thousands of acres and parks of minor dimensions. I want to be understood now, I do not mean these things should be copied, because man cannot copy, but out of these impressions should grow the thought that creates such work in parks and gardens that is fitting to that section of our Country, fitting to its people, a part of them, their own, their home, their all.

When the sun rises, I can see from this trail over the blue waters the rosy down of morning creeping over the great wilderness which is Canada. I can see the sun set over the rolling lands of Michigan and Wisconsin, and when the horizon breaks out into its glorious colors, reflecting the last rays of the setting sun, I know that it is then lighting up the great plains to the west of me, and I can see the long shadows towards eveningtide lying over the prairies of Nebraska and the Dakotas. From this trail one catches the play of the mysterious northern lights, and sees the trail of the silvery moon across the sea, and the deep blue of starry heavens reflected in the waters. Dark and mysterious cliffs, facing the storms of millions of years, rise abruptly out of the sea, still challenging the tempest and relating the story of untold ages in their determination to be. The hand of the Great Master, the Great Architect and Artist, has here been at work and has given us humans the opportunity of grasping His great Message. Here is visioned what is fitting for a people, the worthwhile for a better and a more intelligent life. Man's work, followed generation after generation has all the faults and mistakes of mankind. It, like the giant tree of the forest, decays and like the tree's great trunk, that slowly develops into a new world, man's work must be reborn; but its rebirth must come from the bosom of mother earth of which it is a part. There is no limit to the ideas, to the various plans nature has given to work with so the compositions become one of nature and man, or God and man. And wherever this Unity has been completed, great accomplishments have resulted, remaining throughout the ages. We are fortunate, indeed, in our country of having the primitive close at hand. And the tendency of today is to preserve that which has been given us. An understanding of our native landscape is growing, but we are still far from the goal. The many, even those who are learned but who have grown up on the pavement of our cities know little about it.

Parks and gardens are living examples of the cultural life of a people. They must speak the truth and they must be built on love. Show and pretense, selfishness and barabaricism have no place in these works of art, the finest of all arts. Each plant has its own life to live and should be allowed to express that life to its greatest measure.

I love to see the plants come out of mother earth with their tiny hands stretching for the spring sun. I like to see them grow and give of their bloom and their beauty in flowers and perfume, and I like to see them in the winter landscape, especially those with seed pods or tassels and silvery heads. I love the purple heads of sumac as I see them now out of my window, stretching their heads out of four feet of snow. How colorful they appear in the white setting, and how much joy they add to the winter landscape with the temperature in the figures of the arctic.

A garden of variety and novelty, flowers packed in like sardines in a box, discarded when they are through blooming, has no spiritual worth. It is more in the material, something that should never be introduced by the gardener who must have a higher spiritual ideal of things, who must be a leader of his people in his particular art. There are many, too many following the other course who must be educated and led into the right trail. That is the purpose of the garden maker and not to play to the galleries for the sake of dollars, but to play to the soul and the spirit of men for the joy that it brings to them.

I am opposed to clipped hedges and clipped trees of any kind (I am not referring to fruit trees that are planted only for economic purposes, but to plants that have a beauty of their own and should be allowed to express that beauty). The greatest pity of it all is, the landscapor, or gardener, follows the architect, has no faith in his own power, his own creative work, or he would not submit to such distortions, such cruelty, such barbaric tendencies. I prefer a stone wall or a brick wall, if a wall has to be. Clipped hedges, imitating the more secure structure, deforming plants, has, to me, no place in the evolution of things for a higher life on this earth. It is a false thing and not a product of a mind that wants to guide his people on a secure trail fitting to their life and thoughts far into the future.

The foreigner is still the gardener in America. He has carried his thoughts from his home lands, wherever he was born, and planted them in his adopted country, quite a menace to his new home. But not purposely—he did his best. Our schools are permeated with the ideas of Europe. There is little native thought, little native accomplishment.

I shall never forget one lovely evening, giving advice to a Park Commission in the State of New York, coming down one of the hilly slopes over Central New York. Below me lay a valley in evening light, peaceful and serene. Every farmstead and every village as we saw from above, was hidden in a crown of gold, the golden heads of the sugar maple now in glorious colors of autumn. When the pioneer came to Central New York there were no railroads, there were no nurseries. Buildings had to be built out of the rocks and the trees on the land. The pioneer women had a love for beauty and to satisfy this love they went out into the forests surrounding their new homes and dug saplings, maple saplings, and planted them around their farmsteads, in their villages and on their burial places. That was more than one hundred fifty years ago, but the beauty they created still lived and was in its prime of life as I viewed it from the hillside that evening; a beauty I have never seen anywhere equal to in my country. It shows what is fitting, what expresses the best in our country and sings the song we sing.

Wherever we are, whether in the mountainous regions of the Atlantic Coast, on the coastal plains along the Gulf of Mexico, on the great prairies of Mid-America, or the Pacific slope, each section, if understood, has its own beauty out of which to create what is fitting and what is best for its people. We can create a beautiful land in this way, only, each section singing its own tune and its own love for native land. And what a rich world it would be if we, for once, could stop this imitating each other.

Just think! an Italian garden in America! where the noble cypress and stone pine that influenced its creation cannot grow, and the short lived Lombardi Poplar takes their place. And the attempt at garden making in California, where there exists a rich flora, a wealth of beauty that is perhaps not found elsewhere in the world, is laughable. But man has grown in intelligence (?), he has created more and more civilization, but not culture, and culture is the spiritual aspect of man. He shall never garden finely, nor build fitting parks, before he has reached a cultural height demanding them.

Judging the mentality and the intellect of a people from how they build their parks and gardens, our typical commercial civilization has subdued the higher intellect to a degree that there is a tendency of lowering the state of mind to a lesser appreciation and a lesser understanding of the value of what is fine and noble. This seems to be found in every walk of life. If a master has created a park or garden, the danger of mediocracy may follow, as "the-know-it-alls" will soon change a master work to nothing-ness. The craving for show and pretense—to be it—with great examples of the skill and trickery of horticulturalists is much in evidence and has destroyed many a beautiful garden and made park landscapes ridiculous and grotesque. It is the simple things in life that count, that fit and speak an eloquent language. But those who have become possessed with the complex of gold have lost this feeling. City Parks should bring to those who, with or without their own wishes, have become prisoners of our great cities, to those hundreds of thousands who have little or no opportunity of seeing the lands of their forefathers and of which they are a part, the perfume and the beauty of the living green of their land as it can be expressed and as it will thrive in the city complex. The park in the city has also the purpose of bringing in light and air into the city complex, and, that so essential, rest and peace.

Each school should be surrounded with a park so the boy and girl from early youth until it leaves this educational center can come in contact with the living green, the perfume and color of flowers, the refreshing shade of trees and the song of the birds. What a change there would be in the whole life of our people when this bit of native beauty could penetrate into these city homes. The park areas around the schools could also be a place where mother and father could enjoy the starry evenings under the heavens and not be blinded by the electric light that hounds them from evening until dawn.

I want to emphasize the school in the park, the importance in our machine age of this most essential school planning so these schools with their surroundings may appear as oases, as great wedges in a modern city complex, bringing in light and sweet perfume and the song of birds to those that need all this so badly and are otherwise deprived of their rightful heritage. It is vital that every school in our large cities, the world over, should be placed in a park. This medium of a finer life should be a part of all education as it is often of more importance than what the class room has to give.

Only native trees and plants should be used around the school grounds, trees and plants that beautify the homeland and out of which our forefathers saw life. To sit under a tree which might be the noblest tree in the environs and let the thoughts wander beyond the cement walls of the city is a stimulant of great worth to the city boy or girl.

The school parks should be in walking distance of all the people if we desire to break the great masses of concrete and stone and brick, if we desire to tear down the prison walls of our great city.

We speak about a unified American art—this cannot be. We have an extensive Country with many different climates and each section will, naturally, have its own art. We may love our Country as a whole, but we cannot become a people of the same characteristics. Nature will not permit this. Our expressions will be different, but that does not hinder us from becoming a united people with the same national feelings, but our parks and our gardens on the Gulf Coast will have the shade of the Live Oak, those in New England will lie under the shade of elms, in this Mid-Western country the hardwoods will be seen, the giant California trees will speak in the Northwest and the arid plains will have the miniature forest. Each one has a beauty all its own, each one the best for that section in which through years of selection and elimination they have become victors in the struggle. The question may be asked, "why try to express in the parks and gardens of man made world the beauty expressed in the primitive? Why not do different?" The answer is, "a cultural life demands an understanding of this intimate beauty which belongs, which is home, which is ours."

There are certain human accomplishments that have had their influence on my work, and perhaps more than any other, Schubert's "Fifth Symphony," a repetition of a note in an old Bavarian Folk Song. This repetition which I have enjoyed has become a part of my work in a repetition of certain plants throughout the composition, lending themselves to a lyrical note of great charm in the landscape composition.

The motives for parks and gardens exist in great variety, everywhere. Each one different, but equally as beautiful if one but has the eyes and the imagination to see and understand. In a garden which was built in the north on the cold and raw coast of the Atlantic, rather strange country to me, where the landscape was monotonously green from spruce trees, I planted acres of flowers in place of grass. In this cool and humid climate they bloomed almost all summer, whereas, with us in Mid-America they would have lasted but a few weeks. It was a delightful experience and a most satisfactory one—not strange to the country by any means. It became a delightful pallette of colors in a sun opening amidst dark evergreens.

I was building a waterfall in a Chicago park. It was to supply an inland lake so to keep the water constantly at a certain height, and in that way support the vegetation that had been planted on its shores, partly for the play of fish, but largely as a protection against turbulent waves on stormy days. I had just at that time been charmed by the stratified rock of limestone and sandstone here in Illinois along some of our prairie rivers which so far had never been used. My man who had a great imagination and who was very susceptible to the beauty of steep rocky cliffs with their romance and adventure did not seem to grasp my instructions. After numerous attempts of trying to please me, he finally concluded that I had gone insane and so told his wife after I had said if he understood Mendelssohn's Spring Song he would grasp what I wanted. But Mendelssohn's Spring Song, at the request of his wife, he heard. A few days later I came back and the waterfall was finished. It sang the right song, the soft and quiet tones of the great plains of North America and not the turbulent song of the mountain waterfall. Living on the plains one would quite naturally understand the waterfall in that way.

We are so eager to put everything on paper and then from the paper extend it to the land on which the plan has to be developed. What folly! One sees best on the land out of which these shrines of Man's ability and ingenuity has to be built. It takes no learning, no experience to haul in a thousand loads of soil, steal it so to speak from one place and put it in another, but it takes skill and long experience to cultivate poor soil into something that will give sustenance to the plants one uses.

We see miles of land just a mess of weeds and rubbish as an introduction to the gateway of our cities, depleted of soil that has been hauled away into parks and private gardens. I consider it unprofessional, indeed, to do that sort of a thing. But where is the noble profession today in this mechanical age, and where is the artist and the technician who as developed from the earth on which he lives. His spirit has gone to sleep by the influence of gold and material [technique]. Without the spiritual forces within, no great park nor garden can be created, nor any other work of art. We must return to the simpler and more profound things of life. We must plant our feet solidly on mother earth. One great author has said, "beware, you, who plays with soil in which your childhood feet have never trod."

It is not the gaudy, the great exclamation points, the arrogant and selfish that we, if we are imbued with the right sort of thing, must give to our people. It is the things that carry them onward to a higher and finer life, to an understanding, not only of themselves but of kindred folks wherever found; understanding their accomplishments, their desires to create and express themselves in the best way they know how; to admire their work well done, but not to copy, as in that way we are inferior and subservient; to be stimulated and encouraged and then to do that which fits us and in that way express ourselves and get credit for what we do—there lies the honor and nowhere else! When we have succeeded in covering our land, our villages, our towns and cities with the beauty that is ours, we have succeeded in doing what we were destined to do, what the great Master expected us to do, to be one with Him. We have conquered, we have reached the height of a cultural life on this earth, we have done what was expected of us. Much of this I have said may seem like generalities, but it is nevertheless fundamental. Without a greater thought of what we are to do spiritually as well as materially, we can accomplish nothing of our own. As the trail that I described in the beginning sings its own song, so must our parks express the same spirit. They should not be a conglomoration of things like an outdoor exhibit.

The Nordic, or if you please, Germanic mind, is not imbued with formalism of any kind. To him it is an affected thing. It does not speak the truth as the truth should be told by an intellectual people. To hint it is foreign. One of the most fascinating things to the Nordic mind is the fire, the beginning of civilization. I love the fire and I love the council ring, the first of which I constructed back in 1890 in my own garden. In this ring all are on the same level; one is neither greater nor better than his fellow companion. Here each looks the other square in the face. It is the place for close companionship, for song and deliberation. One is free, as the starry heavens above is the ceiling and the mystery and deep shadows of surrounding trees and plants are the walls. Not a definite world, but one that carries the imagination into the primitive of things; and when the blue smoke, curling from the friendly fire, rises heavenwards, there is a note of profound importance.

These council rings are not strange in a park. They belong in some secluded nook, or on the edge of the water where their friendly fire sends greetings to those across the water, or on a hillock where it is partly hidden by trees or kindred plants that permit a gleam of living fire to reach the eyes of those in the distance. I have in mind a council ring I built on a little hillock, surrounded with native crabapples on a carpet of violets. It is a dream land in May when the crabapples are filled with the beauty of rosy flowers and the violets are like a blue sea below, and the air is filled with sweet perfume. It is a privilege to sit and watch the petals of the crabapple fall, one by one, on the blue sea of violets. There is no absence of spiritual worth in such companionship? No book could ever replace the moments spent here.

The park border should reflect the park, and not the city street. I am much inclined to scatter the trees in the parkway, reflecting the forest and not the walls of the city buildings. It makes the imagination wander to a greater world than that which the city represents. I like breaking the parkway with certain small trees, like hawthorn, crabapple, plum, or similar types of plants, or low growing roses. (When I speak of roses I mean native roses and not cultivated forms, often brutal in their big fluffy faces and arrogant colors.)

Large meadows bordered by restricted woodlands and carpeted by millions of native flowers is a note of great strength in the park picture. Shrubbery carpeted with spring beauties, hepaticas, trilliums, or many other of our native woodland flowers is gay in spring and free from this continual disturbance that I presume originally came from cultivation in the nurseries for the sake of quicker growth. Shrubbery likes this sort of an association because it gives it a cool carpet during hot summer days. Can you imagine anything nobler and more refreshing than the golden tassels of the common hazel swaying in the late April breeze over a carpet of spring flowers against the purple trunks of native plums. It is a real spring song. I know no finer. Its tones are finer than the best of our great musical compositions, that is if we can here the tune.

Where the park areas are extensive enough to permit some of the land to be planted solid with trees, representing a forest, a liberal planting of undergrowth that is in harmony with the trees is essential so to enlarge the vision of a limited area and give it the feeling of a forest. This undergrowth produces a lacy touch. It also brings shade which permits shade loving flowers that are rare and timid. Other parts of the forest, if left open, is a haven for mass planting of such plants that love to grow in masses, and bring out wonderful carpets of subdued colors, so much softer than out in the open sunlight. One often sees the mistake of shrubbery planting along the forest border which looks like a wall entirely strange to the rest of the composition. The forest border should be open at intervals so the eye might penetrate into the deep shadows. I often mix with our hardwoods the juneberry (amelanchier). It is one of the fine notes in our hardwood forest and I have learned to know it intimately.

There is one of these juneberries just outside my studio window and it brings the first message of spring. I have seen it in bloom in a snow storm when one could hardly distinguish between the snowflakes and the fleeting blossoms drifting along with the flakes—a real adventure of youth daring the tempest. It made an everlasting impression on me and I have loved this chap ever since. A garden in northern Michigan planted in canoe birch, juneberries and hepaticas grew into a lovely poem.

Trees are friendly. They love companionship, and are more impressive in a group, with their branches interlaced, as they are more happy in that way. They give us humans a lesson we need so badly. I love to see them on a little hillock, expressing some secret note in the landscape, or on the edge of the meadow; or in some point where the last rays of the setting sun illuminates their golden heads in autumn and in that way gives us a glorious picture. The single tree often becomes an arrogant chap, all to itself and out of harmony with its environments. It becomes a forced thing, something on exhibit, something uncalled for in the composition of fine park making.

In most of my work the water usually reflects the prairie river. A pool or a small lake may be lovely but it becomes a thing in miniature and I dislike the miniature. Man is above that sort of thing. A winding waterscape has mystery as one does not know where its source is, nor where it is going. A pool may, however, have its charm and its purpose in a water garden, surrounded by deep shadows, a thing by itself as one sees so many of these glacial sink holes in the woods of Michigan and Wisconsin. It is quite a revelation to wander along the trail through the deep woods, meeting an opening of that kind where a mother duck is paddling across the water, followed by a long line of young ones, amidst the snow white petals of lovely water lilies, disappearing in a forest of cattails, calamus and rushes. Quite frequently the mountain ash and the highbush cranberry have reached the edge of these hidden pools, or perhaps a ridge of moss covered rocks creeps out of a forest of hemlocks or spruce or fir trees. They are sanctuaries of rare beauty, and they are the home of the shy thrush, and what a privilege, from a hidden nook, to listen to this sweet song at sundown. These pools belong in the park if in harmony with their environments.

Only such recreation that puts life into the park landscape should be introduced, and this in a harmonious way. Nothing should come in that distracts from the art of Landscaping which is a fine and as definite in its expression as any other of the fine arts. A park littered with all sort of playground facilities is not a park in my way of thinking, nor does it express any art. Playgrounds belong somewhere else and best of all around the school—and so do the swimming pools and wading pools. But if they cannot be kept out of the park, then they should be located near the streets or thoroughfares where they are easily accessible for those wishing to use them and do not infringe upon the natural beauty of the park.

I do not belittle the importance and the purpose of our modern playgrounds, but I think they are often over-emphasized and to me, the shy violet with its sweet perfume along the hidden trail is of far greater spiritual importance to the boy and girl of our cities than all the playgrounds ever made by man. Great people, great men and women, grew out of the germanic lands long before we knew the [technique] of playground making, and so it will be in the future and forever as long as nordic people live on this earth.

Straight roads do not belong in our parks. These roads are the expression of the city with its straight walls, fine for cannon balls to roar through, but not conducive to stimulating the poetic senses. The curved road has mystery in its make-up. It is a thrill to see something come around the corner and then see it disappear again into the unknown. Such is life itself, expressed in curves.

But curved roads should never be planted with rows of trees. The two do not fit. Straight rows of trees belong along straight streets to form the Gothic Arches which have a charm and a beauty if they are not permitted to subdue the landscape to an architectural mass of rigid lines that seem to strangle the freedom of the spirit.

The automobile has made it necessary to have parking places for those who visit the park in that way. These spaces should be inconspicuous and provided with proper sanitary facilities. They should be located near the boundary of the park, but should not interfere with the street picture. Now the garden should reflect the things I have said about the park. We are not inclined to grow vegetables in our gardens. They are rather inexpensive in the market and our people are provided with means so to buy them. It is only the few that enjoy growing things for the kitchen. I believe, to make a garden complete, there should be included earth, water and rocks, and such plant life that will bring out the associate parts in full harmony with each other. The architectural mind considers the garden only a decorative thing. He plants the tree or flower or shrub in an impossible place so to satisfy his idea or his vanity. These plants live but a short time as cripples, then they are ruthlessly thrown out. Such a garden lacks any appreciation for the life that makes a garden and it better not had been. The plant is life as you and I, and life should be respected and given a place where it can be enjoyed and where it can enjoy life. This I emphasize because it is the fundamental note of gardening of a thinking people.

I remember an incident in a large garden. A border of zinnias had been planted on either side of the path to the kitchen garden. My friend wanted to show me the beauty of these zinnias which were planted for cut flowers for her home. As we reached the end of the path, my friend bent down, got ahold of a beautiful red zinnia and tore it out and threw it ruthlessly away. The other zinnias were all a bluish shade. This little chap had somehow got into the wrong place. I asked her, "why did you do that? What right had you to destroy a plant that was enjoying God's sunshine and that gave me a real thrill as I saw it in the distance while coming down the path? He had no chance?"

One often makes the mistake of planting too many large trees in the allotted space. I have never objected to a fruit tree of some kind, more for the sake of the blossom than the fruit. In my garden is a hawthorn tree. The stratified outstretched grey branches of this hawthorn express the horizontal lines of our great plains of North America, and it is on the plains we can see its friendliness and its beauty, not on the hillsides, nor in the woodlands, but on the edge of the prairies where it lights up the landscape in winter and brings such beauty with its snow white flowers in springtime, and later with its red berries gives food for the birds. It is not too large for any garden. I have often said that such a tree, with a little pool for the birds to bathe in, with a few moss covered rocks, a few flowers, and a bit of green turf, is a complete garden. Other gardens might be more gigantic in size, more showy, and of a different motive, but they can be no more complete and no more expressive.

Invariably, I will use a bit of turf in planning a garden. It expresses the plains. It is a part of our landscape, the long horizontal lines disappearing on the far horizon. It is the plainsman's vision and it is a part of practically every garden I have made in our great prairie country. Sometimes, as I have before mentioned, it may be all, it may be a mixture of grass and flowers, like our prairie violets and other plants that are low, so when the grass gets tall, it can be cut without disturbing the flowers in any way.

I mentioned before that I introduced the sedimentary rock to our gardens back in 1890. Since then it has been used so profusely that beautiful gardens have turned into stone piles, cold and uncompromising, ridiculous in their composition—rocks everywhere. Some kinder souls try to overcome this barbaric introduction with carpets of flowers, trying to hide the rocks when each stone should have a message of its own. The introduction of rocks must be a part of the garden and not a thing by itself demonstrating arrogance and an absolute foreign expression entirely out of tune with the rest of the garden. Rocks are most beautiful when covered with moss and lichens, with a few flowers that love to live in the crevasses and here express their beauty more than anywhere else. They should represent a quiet place with refined lines, not a pile of rocks with no expression, no charm, no poetry.

The garden should never be a museum or a botanical collection with a riot of colors that makes one turn to drink. It should be a sanctuary, a church, if you please, where one can sit and enjoy lovely things in a quiet and secluded spot. And how the birds love such a spot! And what a joy it is to watch them pick the food from the feeding table, or take a bath in the little pool, later to be rewarded by their sweet song amongst apple blossoms and kindred things.

I do not like arbors because they have to be replaced from time to time, and the plants that grow over them more or less destroyed at that time. I had a problem once of providing shade in a little court. I solved it by moving a large apple tree into the center of the court. The apple tree fitted; it was domestic. Its lovely pink flowers of spring and its lovely fruit of summer gave joy to my client and her friends. It gave all the shade that was needed and there were no walls to prevent the cool breezes from coming in. The chairs could be moved as one pleased. Here was freedom not found in an arbor.

In the Lincoln Memorial Gardens at Springfield, Illinois, the plan originated entirely from the thought that the land selected for this purpose should not be changed. It should be made to express its own beauty and the strength of the character that was Lincoln, our great statesman, our great liberator, the man who wrote the "Gettysburg Speech" (the finest oration ever printed in the English language) whose home for many years was Springfield, so that the spirit of this great man would become a part of the garden. It should express his life more than the monumental statuary and buildings erected in his honor, buildings and monuments that will long be in dust when the white oaks, the acorns of which were planted last spring, will still sing the song and speak of his memory on the little hillocks on Lake Springfield, in Illinois.

The land consists of rather rolling prairie land, where during ages the water had cut its way down to the lower levels. This is now an inland lake formed for the purpose of giving water to the people of the city of Springfield. Originally it was small brooks, contributaries to the larger Sangemon River flowing through the city. Beyond the shores of the lake is the prairie landscape of Illinois, so from these hillocks; or higher elevations, the view goes far into Illinois country. A few scattered trees remained of what was once forested land. It is along our streams in the prairie country that woodlands are found and nowhere else. The depressions, or run-offs, were left open. The hillocks were covered with trees, trees native to Illinois, but what is native to that section of Illinois is also native to all states that Lincoln had lived in. The lower levels along the margin of the lake were planted with thousands of meadow flowers, like phlox, buttercups, and a host of others; and the shoreline was planted with iris and calamus and cattails to keep the shoreline from being washed by turbulent waves in stormy weather as well as for ornamentation. It is the best protection I have ever found and which I always use in making lakes in parks and private estates.

The level lands of the garden have been left as sun openings, prairies covered with the prairie phlox, while the larger and taller flowers such as our giant sunflower and others fringe the woodlands. Here you will find great masses of black-eyed-susans, purple corn flowers, asters, golden rods, etc.; along the lanes, the more shadow loving flowers; and in the woodlands carpets of woodland flowers. The lanes which sometimes measure thirty to forty feet, sometimes less, have groups of small trees such as hawthorn, crabapple, flowering dogwood, planted in groups so the eye might penetrate the depths of the woodlands at intervals. These lanes have special names, the names of the trees that are used to express them. The purpose of these lanes is to show the plants as one sees them in masses on the edge of the prairie landscape so they might express in a way the greatness of our prairie country out of which grew this great statesman. Here in the United States, and especially on the great open plains, we think in big terms. The plains are vast, thousands of miles in extent and this makes our whole mental scale large and this scale must go into our gardens and parks. They must express the expanse which is the United States of America. There are no paths of gravel or asphalt or other material in this Lincoln Garden. The paths are woodland trails and the lanes have a cut green turf—that is to say where you are permitted to walk, the rest is in flowers. It had to be this way or the harmony of that sort of a garden would have been destroyed by the introduction of sharp definite edges of path or roads.

For gathering places, places to rest, there are council rings. Some of these rings are on the edge of a hillock, or down near the water's edge where their friendly fires may send greetings across the lake, way into Illinois country. Some are hidden in the woodlands where their mysterious smoke invites those who come along the road to a friendly fire, sending a glint of bright rays through the tree trunks into the surrounding country as an invitation to partake of its warmth and its inspiring light. On one of the most prominent hillocks of the garden is placed the Lincoln Council Ring in a setting of white oaks, the most noble and inspiring tree that grows in Illinois soil. The parking spaces are placed along the highway, so no cars can penetrate the peace and solemnity of this garden.

The entrances are decorated with great boulders, rocks that have been tossed by the ice masses for thousands of years, formed into a shape weighing many tons. They belong to the plains and they perhaps represent the character of Lincoln better than anything else that has been done in his memory. Along the highway which skirts the garden are colonies of crabapples, prairie roses with scattered trees of sugar maple and white oak. These plants just mentioned form one of the finest compositions in the deciduous landscapes of our country, and it is out of that sort of landscape that great minds have developed, that great men and great women have come, and will come as time goes on.

I am inclined to think we are becoming too much involved in the coarser productions. I say coarse, and I mean it. Nature expresses its serene beauty in the hidden nooks, not in gorgeous display, but in delicate compositions. The little cardinal flower hiding its face in the rushes along the little brook, or on the edge of a swamp; or the red Indian pink in the deep shadows of a ravine and the crevasses of a rocky cliff are outstanding notes of nature. We have become too civilized, materially speaking, and lost the spiritual power of a finer life. We must return to the finer things or decay. Our work as garden and park makers must lead to that goal or it is worthless and better not done.

I often think of a garden made years ago in the heart of Old Kentucky. Something happened, some discord in the family. My client left the old homestead for other parts of our country. I came there as a visitor a good many years later, accidentally so. I found the old place. The ruins of the house that burned down were still in evidence. One of my students was with me. I said to my friend, "let us follow this cow path and see where it leads." We followed it and we came upon one of the pools in a low depression that once had been a marsh. We kept on following the path until we got into a clearing and there was the old swimming hole with its rocky face now covered with green mosses and the redbud and flowering dogwoods, and the red cedars in the depths of the ravine. It had been left unmolested, just as I had planned it years ago. The water in the pool was as clear as crystal as it was spring water that filled the pool. The little clearing of green turf had been left, due to the grazing of cattle. We went beyond and we found ourselves out on the road where the car was waiting for us. My young friend said, as we entered the automobile, "that must have been a terrible shock to you." I answered him, "no, it was a great pleasure, it was a great reward to see that the hand of man had disappeared into the bosom of old Kentucky. I had been true to my calling."

That is the way that all gardens should disappear so that others might have the opportunity of creating their own gardens, fitting to their life, with a mind free from the sins and mistakes of their forefathers. What does it matter if my hand is seen no more in this Kentucky garden, my spirit is there and will remain there as long as the things that my hand planted live, and that is the reward.

The snow lies deep, the old trail is hidden and its secret plant life well protected from winter's cold blast, to greet us again when spring comes over the land once more. It is a delight to put on your snow shoes or ski and pay me a visit over the winding road which dates back to lumbering days, now almost covered with trees bending heavy with snow, beating your face as you move along. I am wondering whether the inspiration of this winter day, sliding along on snow shoes, is not equally as great as later when the snow has left and the earth starts to produce its wealth of beauty once more, or when moonbeams play on the birch trees lighting up the path like so many candles in the deep shadows of the forest, or when the dogwoods and the shad and bird cherries and kindred plants are in bloom, and the forest floor is covered with thousands of trilliums like butterflies flitting over the forest floor, with hepaticas and dogtooth violets forming dense carpets of beauty. Let us make our parks and gardens so that their charm and their inspiring power for those to whom they belong will be equally as good at all seasons of the year, giving thoughts and stimulating man into a finer and better life on this earth.

PROTECT DEVIL'S LAKE BEAUTY

The Capital Times, November 5, 1940

I had a letter from Baraboo the other day, complaining about the destruction of the natural beauty of Devils lake. It is years ago I last visited that beautiful region, and the destruction had begun then. At that time I registered my protest to the Conservation commission and to the governor.

Devils lake and its surroundings are one of the few outstanding monuments in Mid-America, and as such belongs to all the people of this great Midwestern empire. It is a shrine of vast cultural importance. That man still assumes superiority to these magnificent creations shows plainly our state of intellect.

I would like to ask the Conservation commission why they are willing to function under a false name, leading our people into a false understanding of what conservation really means. Why not fly under your true flag so those who are true conservationists are not confused and deceived into thinking we have a conservation policy.

It is about time we, as Americans, woke up to the ignorance of those who have been made the keepers of our great natural scenery and demanded a different course in the management. It is our duty to demand that these places of primitive beauty are kept free from man's interference for unborn generations.

To understand the great message of nature, to find for oneself its hidden secrets, to climb to the top of a high precipice for a vision of the grandness of one's native land, and deep silence keep, as an appreciation for that privilege, is the essence of a strong and sturdy manhood and womanhood. And did we not set these bits of primitive America aside so they might be untouched for future generations to inspire them to greatness and grandeur?

Let me add this: They are most essential for their very existence. Any race that has become too smug and easy to tolerate these God-given shrines in their original state, has died.

Let us awake to our land's full glory before it is too late, before we become soft and unfit to maintain even our freedom.

Let us be ashamed to ride to a mountain peak in a motor car.

Let us destroy these roads that are a mockery to true civilization and climb to these peaks by hand and foot.

Our parks are now cut up with roads for the lazy and self-satisfied. This we do under conservation; I call it exploitation.

These shrines of nature are for the adventurer, and they demand sacrifices amidst nature's mighty forces. To destroy these forces, destroys their message and purpose; and these unadulterated forces are more powerful in molding a people than all the schools or colleges throughout the land. . . .

Shrines were never intended for man to live in, much less play in. The dawn of a new day will appear on the horizon, and we, as a people, will awaken to the spiritual worth of these shrines, to their inspiration and song of courage for youth, to their unchanging story of life when left free from man's interference.

I love to think of little Prince's Pine high on top of the rocky promontory, facing the northwester in a gale of 35 below zero. What a brave little chap, daring the tempest! Then watch him when the spring sun has colored his cheeks. Watch him greeting you in his new dress as beautifully as any flower that grows on this earth of ours, yet as strong and brave as the most daring. He speaks of jubilant youth, courageous, daring, yet bowing his head in humility for the great privilege of life, life well done, a fine symbol for youth to follow.

Conservation has the task of preserving these stories of the infinite so they can be passed on in their true unadulterated form to those that follow throughout the ages.

Conservation must not fail if this land of ours is to remain a fitting place for the growth of men and women as world leaders.

THE CAMP FIRE OR COUNCIL FIRE

Outdoors with the Prairie Club, 1941

The sun has gone below the horizon and put the heavens afire.

It is the great council fire of the spirits of departed Indians.

In the long ago, firebirds brought the fire from the sun to the earth, and the children of the earth joined hands in dance around the fire to thank the firebirds for their great gift.

The druids gathered around their fire, and the Northmen celebrated the departure of their dead chiefs by sending them to sea a flame illuminating the darkness of the far North.

The pagan North lit fires for worship.

These fires are still lit in the Christian North.

Almost extinct, they have been revived with a different meaning.

Around them gather old and young in song and ceremony. They have become a national feast of great value.

Then fires have been worshiped from early times, in almost every part of the earth, but perhaps nowhere more generally than in the North, where the light and warmth always have been welcome.

The American Indian built his fire for peace and for war, and likewise the pioneers gathered around their fires.

We of today have our fires too, and they are blazing up everywhere throughout our country. More and more young and old gather around the camp fire for play and inspiration. It is the most democratic gathering on earth, one man is [no] more than the other, [they] all are on the same level. It is a distinct message for us, for it brings back to our minds the struggles and the life of all mankind from all times.

To us the camp fire has a new meaning. In it we find the joys and the sorrows of the pioneers, their struggles, their hardships, their determination to succeed.

We see, with John Muir, a whole world of things as when he said at his first camp fire: "This is the heat of many summers' suns."

It is, as it were, pioneer life over again; a life close to the soil and of the soil, where we may take counsel with ourselves and with the great spirit, a life that every American must keep as a sacred heritage.

Nowhere is the council fire more inspiring than amongst the trees.

Here we perceive the mystery of God's great out-of-doors, in the dark shadows and depth of darkness that surrounds us.

Here this fire becomes a friend indeed that ever hugs close to us with its flame leaping heavenward, uniting heaven and earth, as it were.

Then under the dark shadows of noble trees, centuries old, we behold the shrine of God's out-of-doors.

The sun is setting brilliantly, it sinks below the purple ridges.

And now the heavens are aflame, blood red.

It is the camp fire of the spirits of the pioneers.

LEARNING THE LESSONS OF NATURE

The Capital Times, September 3, 1942

They say you have to learn as long as you live. My friends tell me I have lived long enough for two lifetimes, but I still have many things to learn. A close association with the soil has taught me that there is always a new lesson for the morrow.

In going to and from our vegetable garden, I pass by a colony of mint with a soft lavender flower. Its spicy delicacy, with the morning dew still fresh upon its blossom, is beyond description. (All worthwhile things are beyond description.) These mints are a friendly sort as they share their food with the field grasses. On first discovering the colony, I moved some of them to a vacant spot near our school building. To my surprise, the plants revolted, becoming a weedy looking patch alongside the school. The liveliness they expressed in the open field was gone. I had ignored their friends, the grasses, amidst which they had made their home.

In moving the mint to this new environment, I had ignored its spiritual message and, had only tried to reproduce its showy side. In removing its finer quality, that of sharing with others, I destroyed its beauty.

Although I discovered years ago that the same principle that makes for beautiful living in the human world holds true all though creation, I still will make these grave mistakes that only experience can remedy.

To sense and to understand the God given message of the children of nature takes a lifetime of seeking, but in the seeking of these messages, the sleeping spark is awakened within us. Nature inspires, never displays!

A little north of Ellison Bay lies a swamp through which passes the main highway. In these mid-summer days the roadside is gay with flowers, sedges, and cattails, and yet in its gayety, there is nothing showy nor gaudy in the arrangement. It stimulates the creative, and not the possessive urge.

We who live in a country where the summer resorter pays his yearly visit, see how few of our visitors stop and drink in this message, or even know it is here. They seek our countryside because they need the imagination and freedom their cities cannot give, and when they are here, they close their eyes and ears to all but that which they are used to in their walled-in city home.

They bring with them their lectures, with slides of flowers that can be seen in living form just off their hotel porch. Amidst nature's garden, they produce a flower show, the gaudiest flower getting a prize to satisfy the ego of its owner.

Here lies the root of all wars. The world will never be able to destroy the evil of competition before this word is cleared from our thinking. In a world of real enthusiasm for understanding and accomplishments, this awakening in us of a finer perspective and the will "to be" need not be given to us in this pink pill fashion.

Nature's glorious beauty has so much to teach, but a mind stagnant with city superficiality is bored unless these great wonders are frosted with the sugar of materialism.

In Count Tolstoi's "What is Art," he speaks about the "art that belongs to my class, the type that must be learned because it follows set rules laid down by us who pay for it."

"This," he states, "is deceiving ourselves, as it has no connection with art. Art springs from the soul of man and a true work of art is understood by all mankind as it touches that inner feeling of which we are a part."

And I add to his thought:

"To adulterate the story of Nature, making it speak our language, is to destroy the very foundation of our being, as here is the hand of the Master of all arts."

During one's lifetime there are but a few days that remain on the horizon of memories. Such a day came to me last week when we motored off of the peninsula into the free county of grain fields.

Since Door county has become an orchard county, it has lost much of the charm it possessed when I first laid eyes upon it. Now the monotony of cherry trees has transgressed upon its symphony of open fields bordered by woodlands, sky, and water. (And the problem of harvesting these cherries has brought into Door county the unwholesome atmosphere of transient pickers, which is a sad story for any community wherever this condition has been created. Some day I presume all of these problems will be solved so the aesthetic and material life will go hand in hand. In the meantime one is always trespassing on the other.)

Harvest is the time of contentment for rural folks, and those who go country-wards at this time sense the profound purpose of the land and grasp the contentment of their rural neighbors.

Joyously we went forth, but more joyfully we returned, filled with the satisfaction that we had seen a true expression in the art of living. Miles of colorful fields greeted our eyes, herds of grazing cattle, and the ripened grain in shock ready for harvesting.

We returned home feeling we had felt the hand of man and Nature, working together in complete harmony with each other. Door county's charm of birch trees and rugged cliffs is greatly enhanced by knowing that just south of us lies a vastness of fertile soil which is capable of feeding the multitudes. The early pioneers who settled there smelled this richness and built accordingly. The homes are still standing to testify to their ability and faith.

But the hand of their descendant does not show that same faith as there is but little improvement beyond that which was left by those who turned the first soil. Are they losing the vision that a true sense of the soil gives a people?

In a few days calm will once again lie over the northern part of this peninsula. Our summer visitors will have returned to their city homes.

I am wondering what new knowledge they have reaped this summer to carry home that will be for the betterment of that home environment?

THESE ARE DAYS OF REBIRTH

The Capital Times, May 8, 1943

I have often wondered why our pioneer homesteaders disliked trees so much. One often finds throughout the rural country farmsteads completely barren of any trees, the home standing out with no protecting arms to tie it to the earth of which it is a part, no connecting link between man and the soil from which he reaps his existence.

But it is gratifying to see that these pioneer's children have profited by the mistakes of their forefathers and are planting young saplings around the home so that in some future years the comfort and loveliness that only trees can bring into the home will be not only theirs but also those who follow them. Trees are man's true friends, and you can rest assured that where trees grow, there man can live also. They give him shelter in winter and cooling shade on hot summer days, and when a shimmer of green appears in their tops in early spring they awaken man to life anew. They bring an atmosphere of friendliness to the home, to the town and to the village, and nowhere in the world is this spirit of friendliness as forceful as in the small towns and villages scattered throughout our land.

Under the protecting arms of overarching trees these small communities assert themselves as cultural bearers of our people. These towns speak of true neighborliness, and as long as we do not get too far removed from the freedom and the breadth these small towns suggest, there will be no danger of our vision being warped and stunted. The home that is graced by the protecting arms of overarching trees is one of rest and repose, and is a friendly welcome to the visitor.

The earth is now pregnant with growth, as it is growing time. Work is starting in the fields and gardens, and each new day the revelation of new growth is visible, and a shimmer of green is appearing where only a few days ago was mud and the browned vegetation of the previous year. These are days of rebirth, and the good earth is telling the story of life everlasting, of life without interference.

What tragedies are written in the history of time because man tries to interfere with the continual procession of life! What suffering man brings upon himself because he tries to fit this life into his limited sphere rather than fit himself into life's sphere! Families, and peoples, and nations have disappeared because they did not learn this great lesson before they were swallowed-up into oblivion.

To prepare the soil, to sew the seed, to watch it grow, and later to reap the harvest, tells the full story of life. The knowledge man receives from his garden of the succession of life is the most sound and the least adulterated of any knowledge he receives. It broadens his vision to true neighborliness.

When an understanding of the fleeting beauty of growing things takes its proper place in the education of the growing mind in our educational system, we shall need have no further fear for the welfare of our people. Their feelings will be quickened by a sound judgment where lust and greed will find no room for stagnation and decay.

Our children are entitled to the great knowledge this living world has to offer them. With a little guidance and help at the very beginning, before their mind is stuffed to the strangulation state with unfounded theories, our youth will expand and grow as freely and as easily as the tiny plants that are now breaking the crust of mother earth, peeping out into the sunlight to grow into an inherent beauty.

They will be individuals in a true co-operation. They will unloose the shackles of license and take on the responsibility of freedom. They will think the democratic way, respecting the rights of their neighbors, throwing off suspicion which leads to strict laws and a rigid social order, and will take their place in the friendly order of things.

They will not only become individuals, but will also recognize the fact that the world is a nucleus of individuals. Man and nature, working together in one harmonious whole, brings to light these great fundamental principles which are necessary for man to keep the democratic way alive.

Flowers are a wayshow'er to a neighborly spirit, a feeling the whole world must find before we can have a lasting peace. Flowers at the door to greet the visitor is the most friendly welcome we can give our visitor. And when I think of the friendliness of flowers, I remember an incident that happened during the first World war.

A friend and I were travelling on a North Western train between Chicago and Green Bay when our discussion of the war ended in a violent disagreement. We looked askance at each other. Suddenly we noticed hundreds of lilies which had been spared along the railroad right-of-way by the road officials; and we both started to smile, becoming friends again.

Of what value is our great advancement in the sciences and our so-called improved ways of living if we lose sight of our kindred spirit and the living beauty which keeps this spirit alive? It is most important that in our scientific march forward not one ounce of living beauty is sacrificed on the scales of what we call human progress.

Strides made by us that ignore life itself are only a move in the wrong direction and must someday be retraced. Life is the essence of all the arts, the sciences, and human progress, and growth is the exemplification of life pure and unadulterated.

"Who can realize the supple power and the emotional forces that lie hidden in the misty bloom of the witch-hazel in the purple shadows of the dying day?"

THE "WHY" OF PARKS AND WILDERNESS AREAS

Lands for State Parks, December 1946

Civilized man has always been attracted and inspired by the wilderness, by that part of mother earth not touched by him. The wilderness is a strange world to him and his curiosity and love for the unknown urges him to explore and to seek the hidden secrets expressed in its unfathomed depths. The harmonious peace of the wilderness in contrast with man's daily life in his own made cities of confusion and disharmony soothes his overworked nerves and fills him with a spiritual outlook on life. But usually an eagerness for this newly discovered way of life on the part of many turns out to be destructive to the wilderness in which it is found, for when man decides to live in the wilderness, that wilderness disappears. Modern man in the mass cannot have the wilderness and live in it too!

One of the greatest problems of today is the instilling of a love for the beauty of native land, a desire to listen to the primitive and to bury our roots deep into native soil. A guiding hand from those that have been blessed with a love for this God made beauty of the earth is needed, to prevent us from destroying the very thing that has been found essential for a more wholesome life.

Much of that part of Wisconsin nearest to its principal centers of population has more and more developed into a summer vacation land. Year by year those areas unfit for agriculture, and which represent the only wilderness left in that part of our State, are fast disappearing under the hand of the vacationist who comes because of these wilderness areas, not realizing that the very wilderness that brought him here is being destroyed by him. When the wilderness is gone, he will follow it, seeking farther away for what he once found a few miles from home. The day is close at hand when the last remnant of primitive America along the shore of Lake Michigan will be a memory, and the thing that attracted the tourist and the vacationist be gone forever unless something is done, and done now, to prevent such a calamity. And the cultivated lands in this part of the State also need these forested areas for protection. The soil is such that without these border lands of wilderness area the cultivated fields will revert to desert waste, thus forcing the farmer to leave for better lands elsewhere. The ax is singing through our woodlands every winter. Soon our wilderness woodlands will be a thing of the past. We have arrived at the crossroads. Which way are we going?

Eastern and southeastern Wisconsin has little left of those lands where one still can see the footprints of pioneer and Indian before him, where native vegetation can be found dating back to the time when ice covered the most of our State; however, giant elm trees that were struggling saplings when Columbus first saw America, are now five to six feet in diameter and towering over the rest of the forest, acres of arctic wild flowers indigenous to these regions, still thrive in a few places on Wisconsin soil.

Of remaining tracts along the Lake Michigan shore, the dunes country south of Jacksonport, and the Mink River country and adjacent lands, including Europe Lake and the low cliffs along the shores of Lake Michigan where are found evidences of pre-historic times in the fossils imbedded in the rocks and where the far away view over billowing waves reminds one of the breadth of Mid-America, the land of great promise, are the most important wilderness areas to be preserved from destruction. True, the bark of the coyote and the cry of the wildcat is no more in these areas, and where formerly great flocks of wild ducks settled, there now are none; the honk, honk of the Canadian goose is a rarity; the majesty of the swan soaring the sky has not been seen for years; the eagles are rarely seen silhouetted against the blue sky; the deer, the partridge and the pileated woodpecker are fast following. But there are a few last stands of wilderness left where man can find his way back through untold ages. Shall these, too, be sacrificed to indifference and carelessness; shall the youth of our land for untold generations to follow be denied these last remnants of their rightful heritage? Shall we, through greed and wanton destruction, approve the destruction of the last bits of infinite beauty that charmed our forebears and made them courageous and far visioned?

There is a real thrill to sail down the Mink River which is still hedged in by the primitive forest, on the edge of which the great blue heron is seen fishing; to fish in the deep clear water which abounds with pike and bass. One here can feel man's dominion over this world not made by hands and which inspires a trust in man and urges him on to noble deeds.

In periods when man's world roars with destruction and uncertainty, and the voices of life and growth and man's ascendancy is drowned, the wilderness must be there to quiet the storm and lead man back to where he once again can hear life's purpose. May our love for all creation, for its infinite beauty and true purpose, guide us into a right reverence for this world not of our making so we will see to it that unborn generations will have the right to drink at this fount.

THE HEAT OF MANY SUMMERS' SUN

The Capital Times, December 10, 1947

Sitting in the warmth and glow of the open fire at eventide, I think of John Muir's words on his first night in the High Sierras by the campfire, "the heat of many summers' sun!"

Many summers' sun, many winters' snow, many springs' rains, have played their all important part in giving the glow now reflected from the hearth to my all absorbing senses. Through time untold through life's continuous surging from a tiny seed to a towering oak, the warmth of many summers' sun has been carefully stored to bring forth warmth in time of need. And as the flickering firelight plays upon my surroundings, first up on a chair, then on a nearby table, then radiating across the room to a cot in a darkened corner, I think about man's needs since time began; from the aboriginal down through the ages to present man, and I find man has grown in enlightenment where the forests of the earth have furnished an environment of spiritual grandeur.

The Clearing, situated on these rocky cliffs of Green Bay, is surrounded by the forests aspiring grandeur, and time and again I have heard students of The Clearing express themselves, "I feel taller amidst these trees."

Amidst nature's giants, I find man looks upward in place of downward when he meditates, he looks forward rather than backward. A mighty oak, a motherly elm, a poetic birch, a friendly maple all speak to man's finer senses and helps awaken him to his noble heritage.

Along an Indian trail of bygone days I discovered an old weatherbeaten oak tree. The centuries that passed it by have left their mark. Storms and fire have retarded its growth in its long journey upward, but its head was erect and nobly silhouetted against the blue sky. Year after year its golden head of thousands of blossoms swinging to and fro in a fresh May breeze sings the song of spring, its rebirth as it were.

For centuries man has walked this trail and stopped under this oak for cooling shade and friendly greeting. The old trial has now become a highway. So to make way for our present demand for speed it has become less intimate than yesterday. The old oak still stands, but the hurrying throng passes it by with an indifferent glance as though it little belonged to their world or their way of thinking, little realizing that this oak is a part of their connecting link to life itself.

Destroy the trees; mutilate, hack down, saw up, the forests of the earth and man will soon find his world of reason and spiritual growth sliding into a rut of carefulness indifference. That the tree is an inseparable part of God's creation and one of His most noble gifts to man has been proven by its influence of man's ascendancy. But man has still far to go before he places spiritual satisfaction before material needs. Today beauty is considered women's talk, Christian love is for children; nature in general has only one attraction, the profit it brings. Man in his speed crusade is supreme! He little concerns himself with the day of reckoning. His deeds are visible along our highways, in our parks, in our National Reserves where men of broad scope of past centuries set aside nature's unmolested lessons that we today might be blessed with the vision exemplified therein.

In the mature tree's body is stored the record of the years it has lived, reflecting life's continuity, an all important lesson in this day of confusion and uncertainly. One wonders about God's marvelous ways when viewing nature's ways. To see a giant oak tolerate in a friendly way the little Mayflower, as we call it, which hugs close to the oak's roots for winter protection, brings to us a lesson of life's true workings. To know these lessons is man's first essential in seeking to find himself and his place in a benevolent pattern.

In a trip into the eastern sections of our country last summer, I felt the beneficent value of trees along our highways. It was a hot summer day and the sun was merciless. Here and there an early pioneer who had had a love for trees had planted them along the roadways. How soothing these now mature trees felt as we passed them by. The inner urge to speed over the highway, to get through with the journey, disappeared into a feeling of contentment and peace at these points. And the highway itself became an inspirational play of light and shadow under these century-old overarching trees.

Summer or winter, spring or fall, trees give joy that comes from peace and intimate beauty. How often I listen to a chick-a-dee singing from amidst its branches in contrast to the roaring storm.

Trees are the true decorators of this world of ours. They are in scale with the world's magnitude. Recently the hills of our state were covered with the golden foliage of the sugar maple. For a fleeting sojourn it became a new world, a new state. But there are those who would destroy this beauty and autumn glory of our state for personal gain.

Do our schools tell our children about nature's infinite stories and their cultural value to mankind? How many in my section know of the great elms growing here that were large trees when Columbus discovered America. What a privilege to lean your tired body against one of these giant's great trunk and feel its strength surging through you. Do our schools make pilgrimages to these all important connecting links with the past and our future, or do they visit lifeless museums where the living story is destroyed and only mummifications is visible?

In the surrounding woodlands the leaves have now fallen to the ground covering the roots with a warm carpet of exquisite colors under which sleeps a beauty which will awaken again when the sun once again comes higher in the heavens. Light through the trees' bare branches reveals their true form. As I look at their sylvan peace and feel their shelter for cold winter days to come, I think of the goodness of The Great Master in bestowing us with bountiful gifts to satisfy our needs.

Men enjoying the Jensen-designed landscape at the edge
of Chicago's Humboldt Park Prairie River, 1911

NOTES

1. William T. Evjue, "Travelogue: Jens Jensen Wasn't There," *Capital Times*, August 24, 1950.

2. "Jens Jensen Dies; Landscape Expert; Developer of Chicago's Park System Designed Edsel Ford, Rosenwald, Armour Estates," *New York Times*, October 2, 1951.

3. Jens Jensen, *Siftings* (Chicago: Ralph Fletcher Seymour, 1939); Jens Jensen, *The Clearing* (Chicago: Ralph Fletcher Seymour, 1949).

4. Jensen, undated typescript in The Clearing Archives.

5. Jensen, *Siftings* (Baltimore and London: Johns Hopkins University Press, 1990).

6. Jensen, *Siftings, the Major Portion of The Clearing, and Collected Writings* (Chicago: Ralph Fletcher Seymour, 1956).

7. Leonard K. Eaton, *Landscape Artist in America* (Chicago and London: University of Chicago Press, 1964).

8. Robert E. Grese, *Jens Jensen: Maker of Natural Parks and Gardens* (Baltimore and London: Johns Hopkins University Press, 1992).

9. James Jensen, "Transplanting Trees during Mid-Winter," *Park and Cemetery* 8, no. 12 (February 1899): 238–239.

10. Jensen and Ragna B. Eskil used this description in "Natural Parks and Gardens," *Saturday Evening Post* 202, no. 36 (March 8, 1920): 170.

11. James Jensen, "Extermination of the Oak at Lake Geneva, Wisconsin," *Forester* 7, no. 3 (1901): 63–65.

12. James Jensen, "Plan for Hospital Grounds," *Park and Cemetery* 7, no. 10 (December 1901): 185–186.

13. James Jensen, "Topiary Gardening," *Park and Cemetery* 12, no. 5 (July 1902): 320.

14. Ibid.

15. James Jensen, "Parks and Politics," *Park and Cemetery* 12, no. 8 (October 1902): 383–384.

16. Ibid., 384.

17. Jensen wrote the following during this period: "Topiary Gardening," "Parks and Politics," "Marring the Landscape," "Planting Plan for a Cemetery Lot," "Urban and Suburban Landscape Gardening," "Soil Conditions and Tree Growth around Lake Michigan, Part II," and "Hawthorns in the Landscape."

18. Jensen, "Urban and Suburban Landscape Gardening," *Park and Cemetery* 13, no. 1 (March 1903): 1–3.

19. Henry Chandler Cowles, "The Ecological Relations of the Vegetation on the Sand Dunes of Lake Michigan," *Botanical Gazette* 27, no. 2 (February 1899): 27, 97–117, 167–202, 281–308, 361–91.

20. Ervin Zube, "The Advance of Ecology," *Landscape Planning* 18 (1999): 11–29.

21. Jensen, "Soil Conditions and Tree Growth around Lake Michigan," *Park and Cemetery* 14, no. 2 (April 1904): 24–25. "Soil Conditions and Tree Growth around Lake Michigan, Part II," *Park and Cemetery* 14, no. 3 (May 1904): 42.

22. Jensen, "Hawthorns in the Landscape," *Park and Cemetery* 14, no. 1 (May 1904): 3.

23. Ibid., 3.

24. Jensen, "Ideal Edging Plants for Walks and Flower Beds," *Garden Magazine* 3 (April 1906): 136–138.

25. Jensen, "Landscape Art—An Inspiration from the Western Plains," *Sketch Book: A Magazine Devoted to the Fine Arts* 6, no. 1 (September 1906): 21–28.

26. Jensen, *City Club Bulletin* 2 (1908): 11–12.

27. Ibid., 12.

28. Jensen wrote the following during this period: "Some Gardens of the Middle West," "Object Lesson in Placing Park Sculpture," "Concrete Construction in Relation to Park Work," "Beauty and Fitness in Park Concrete Work," and "An Open-Air Exhibition of American Sculpture."

29. Jensen, "Some Gardens of the Middle West," *Architectural Review* 15 (May 1908): 93–95.

30. Jensen, "Improving a Small Country Place," *Illinois Outdoor Improvement Association*, no. 1 (Chicago: Office of the Association, 1910), 10.

31. Jensen, "Regulating City Building," *Survey* 27 (November 18, 1911): 1204.

32. Jensen, *Report to the Woman's League for the Protection of Riverside Park on the Proposed Plan for Changes in the New York Central Railroad along the Hudson* (1916), 1–10.

33. Ibid., 1–2.

34. Jensen, "Testimony Regarding Proposed Sand Dunes National Park," in *Report on the Proposed Sand Dunes National Park, Indiana,* by Stephen T. Mather (Washington: Government Printing Office, 1917), 24.

35. Ibid., 25.

36. Ibid., 50.

37. Jensen, *Report to the Woman's League,* 10.

38. Jensen, *Proposed Sand Dunes*, 26.

39. Ibid., 99–100.

40. Jensen, "Report of Mr. Jens Jensen, Consulting Landscape Architect, on Landscape Design of Columbus Park," in *Forty-Ninth Annual Report of the West Chicago Park Commissioners* (Chicago: West Park Commission, 1918), 16–18.

41. Jensen, "The Naturalistic Treatment in a Metropolitan Park," *American Landscape Architect* 2, no. 1 (January 1930): 34–38.

42. Ibid., 35.

43. Ibid.

44. Jensen, *A Greater West Park System* (Chicago: West Park Commission, 1920).

45. Ibid., 20.

46. Ibid., 45–54.

47. Ibid., 58.

48. Jensen, "I Like Our Prairie Landscape," *Park International*, July 1920, 63–65. Jensen, "Wisconsin Beautiful," *Country Magazine* 14, no. 8 (May 1921): 279–280.

49. Jensen, "Wisconsin Beautiful," 10.

50. Ibid., 10.

51. Ibid., 11.

52. Jensen, foreword to *Proposed Park Areas in the State of Illinois: A Report with Recommendations* (Chicago: The Friends of Our Native Landscape, 1921), 16.

53. Jensen, and Hedwig Fishmann, "Die Landschaftsgäertnerei—eïne Kunst," *Gartenschöenheit* 4, no. 4 (April 1923): 68–69.

54. Ibid., 68.

55. Jensen, "Roadside Planting," *Landscape Architecture* 14, no. 3 (April 1924): 186–187.

56. Jensen, "Highway Beauty," *Roycroft*, March 1924, 26.

57. Jensen, "Novelty Versus Nature," *Landscape Architecture* 15, no. 1 (October 1924): 44–45.

58. Jensen to Genevieve Gillette, April 8, 1942. Gillette worked for Jensen at his office in Ravinia, Illinois, and later helped found a Friends of Our Native Landscape chapter in Michigan.

59. Jensen, "Amerikanische Gartengedanken," *Gartenschöenheit* 6, no. 8 (August 1925): 148.

60. Ibid., 148.

61. Jensen, "The Park Policy," in *A Park and Forest Policy for Illinois* (Chicago: Friends of Our Native Landscape, 1926), 11–25.

62. Ibid., 12.

63. Jensen, "Nature the Source," *Vista* (Urbana: University Landscape Architects' Society, University of Illinois, Spring 1927), 8–11.

64. Ibid., 8.

65. Jensen, "Landscape Appreciation," *Wisconsin Horticulture* 17, no. 9 (May 1927): 129–130, 146–147.

66. Ibid., 129.

67. Friends of Our Native Landscape, *Our Native Landscape* (Madison: Friends of Our Native Landscape, June 1927–May 1934).

68. Jensen, "The Native Beeches in the Chicago Region," *Illinois State Academy of Science Papers in Biology and Agriculture* XXI (February 1929): 69–72.

69. Jensen, "The Naturalistic Treatment in a Metropolitan Park," *American Landscape Architect* 2, no. 1 (January 1930): 34–38.

70. Jensen and Ragna B. Eskil, "Natural Parks and Gardens," 34–38.

71. The Friends of Our Native Landscape and Jens Jensen, *Roadside Planning and Development* (Oak Park: Pioneer Publishing Co., 1932), 3–35.

72. Jensen, "Conservation in the Regional Plan," in *Conference on State & Regional Planning Sponsored by Wisconsin Friends of Our Native Landscape,* April 1934, 26–27.

73. This text is from an undated typescript from the mid-1930s that is attributed to Jens Jensen.

74. Jensen and Camillo Schneider, "Das Haus im Garten ein Gartenheim in Wisconsin," *Gartenschöenheit* 18 (August 1937): 357–359; Jensen and Michael Mappes, "Die 'Lichtung,'" *Die Gartenkunst* 50, no. 9 (September 1937): 177–181; Jensen and Michael Mappes, "Grundsätzliches meiner Park—und Landschaftsgestaltunt," *Die Gartenkunst* 50, no. 9 (September 1937): 182–187.

75. Jensen, "Das Haus," 358.

76. Jens Jensen, "The Nordic's Contribution to America," speech presented at Women's International League for Peace and Freedom, Sixth International Summer School, Provisional Program, Chicago, May 17–31, 1924, 890, 892.

77. Dave Egan and William H. Tishler, "Jens Jensen, Native Plants, and the Concept of Nordic Superiority," *Landscape Journal* 18, no. 1 (Spring 1999): 11–29.

Jensen, late 1940s, at the entry to The Clearing's "cliff house," a rustic retreat built into a bluff facing Lake Michigan that he used for writing and thinking.

Courtesy of The Clearing

BIBLIOGRAPHY

Jensen, James. "Extermination of the Oak at Lake Geneva, Wisconsin." *Forester* 7, no. 3 (1901): 63–65.

———. "Parks and Politics." *Park and Cemetery* 12, no. 8 (October 1902): 383–384.

———. "Plan for Hospital Grounds." *Park and Cemetery* 7, no. 10 (December 1901): 185–186.

———. "Topiary Gardening." *Park and Cemetery* 12, no. 5 (July 1902): 320.

———. "Transplanting Trees during Mid-Winter." *Park and Cemetery* 8, no. 12 (February 1899): 238–239.

Jensen, Jens. "Amerikanische Gartengedanken [American Garden Thoughts]." *Gartenschöenheit* 6, no. 8 (August 1925): 148.

———. "The Camp Fire or Council Fire." In *Outdoors with the Prairie Club*. Chicago: Paquin Publishers, 1941, 352–354.

———. "Conservation in the Regional Plan." In *Conference on State & Regional Planning Sponsored by Wisconsin Friends of Our Native Landscape,* April 1934, 26–27.

———. *A Greater West Park System.* Chicago: West Park Commission, 1920, 9–10, 13–14, three unnumbered pages, 31, 34, 57–59.

———. "Hawthorns in the Landscape." *Park and Cemetery* 14, no. 1 (May 1904): 3.

———. "The Heat of Many Summers' Sun." *Capital Times*, December 10, 1947.

———. "Ideal Edging Plants for Walks and Flower Beds." *Garden Magazine* 3 (April 1906): 136–138.

———. "I Like Our Prairie Landscape." *Park International*, July 1920, 63–65.

———. "Improving a Small Country Place." *Illinois Outdoor Improvement Association*, no. 1 (Chicago: Office of the Association, 1910).

———. "Landscape Appreciation." *Wisconsin Horticulture* 17, no. 9 (May 1927): 129–130, 146–147.

———. "Landscape Art—An Inspiration from the Western Plains." *Sketch Book: A Magazine Devoted to the Fine Arts* 6, no. 1 (September 1906): 21–28.

———. "Learning the Lessons of Nature." *Capital Times*, September 3, 1942.

———. "Marring the Landscape." *Park and Cemetery*, 1902, 200.

———. "The Naturalistic Treatment in a Metropolitan Park." *American Landscape Architect* 2, no. 1 (January 1930): 34–38.

———. "Nature the Source." *Vista*. Urbana: University Landscape Architects' Society, University of Illinois, Spring 1927, 8–11.

———. "The Nordic's Contribution to America." Speech presented at Women's International League for Peace and Freedom, Sixth International Summer School, Provisional Program, Chicago, May 17–31, 1924, 881–892.

———. "Novelty Versus Nature." *Landscape Architecture* 15, no. 1 (October 1924): 44–45.

———. "Object Lesson in Placing Park Sculpture." *Park and Cemetery* 18, no. 9 (November 1908): 438.

———. "Gartengestaltung: Sondervortrag [Garden Design: Special Lecture]." In *Internationaler Gartenbau Kongress, Berlin, 1938*. Berlin: 1939, 1003–1012.

———. "The Park Policy." In *A Park and Forest Policy for Illinois* (Chicago: Friends of Our Native Landscape, 1926), 11–25.

———. "A Program for School of the Soil." Unpublished manuscript, mid-1930s: 66–69.

———. "Protect Devil's Lake Beauty." *Capital Times*, November 5, 1940.

———. "Regulating City Building." *Survey* 27 (November 18, 1911): 1203–1205.

———. "Report of Mr. Jens Jensen, Consulting Landscape Architect, on Landscape Design of Columbus Park." In *Forty-Ninth Annual Report of the West Chicago Park Commissioners* (Chicago: West Park Commission, 1918): 16–18.

———. "Roadside Planting." *Landscape Architecture* 14, no. 3 (April 1924): 186–187.

———. "Soil Conditions and Tree Growth around Lake Michigan." *Park and Cemetery* 14, no. 2 (April 1904): 24–25.

———. "Soil Conditions and Tree Growth around Lake Michigan, Part II." *Park and Cemetery* 14, no. 3 (May 1904): 42.

———. "Some Gardens of the Middle West." *Architectural Review* 15 (May 1908): 93–95.

———. "Testimony Regarding Proposed Sand Dunes National Park." In *Report on the Proposed Sand Dunes National Park, Indiana,* by Stephen T. Mather (Washington: Government Printing Office, 1917), 24–26, 98–100.

———. "These Are Days of Rebirth." *Capital Times*, May 8, 1943.

———. "Urban and Suburban Landscape Gardening." *Park and Cemetery* 13, no. 1 (March 1903): 1–3.

———. "The 'Why' of Parks and Wilderness Areas." *Lands for State Parks.* Madison: Wisconsin State Planning Board, no. 17 (December 1946), 3–4.

———. "Wisconsin Beautiful." *Country Magazine* 14, no. 8 (May 1921): 279–280.

Jensen, Jens, and Ragna B. Eskil. "Natural Parks and Gardens." *Saturday Evening Post* 202, no. 36 (March 8, 1920): 170.

Jensen, Jens, and Hedwig Fishmann. "Die Landschaftsgäertnerei-eine Kunst [Landscape Gardening—An Art]." *Gartenschöenheit* 4, no. 4 (April 1923): 68–69.

Jensen, Jens, and Michael Mappes. "Die 'Lichtung' [The 'Clearing']." *Die Gartenkunst* 50, no. 9 (September 1937): 177–181.

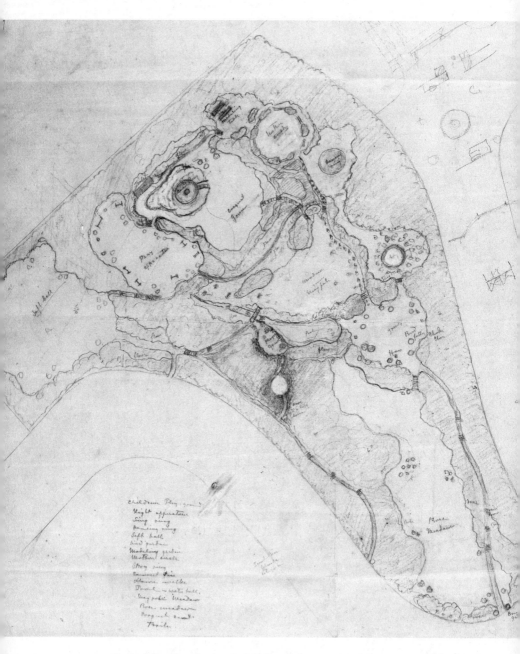

Planting plan for Glenwood Children's Park in Madison, Wisconsin, 1945

WHi Image ID 61542

INDEX

MUSIC COURT

BOAT LANDING

BOAT LANDING

PERGOLA

HITCHING PLACE.

MALL

GARDEN GATE

PROPOSED IMPROVEMENTS
IN
HUMBOLDT PARK

DIVISION ST.